Praise for

India Inc.

"In a sea of global content, few stand out as as influential or as passionate as Vikas Pota, in providing a fresh, new perspective to the subject of India Inc. going global. By telling the stories of some of India's best business brains, this book provides a fantastic insight into how the big challenges of our time are being tackled by the next wave of globally successful entrepreneurs."

S. A. Hasan, Director, TATA Ltd

"An insightful and thought-provoking look at some of the world's top entrepreneurs and how they got there. A must-read for any aspiring Dragon or business person wanting to understand the minds behind the greatest business expansion of our world today."

James Caan, **Dragons' Den**

"Is India going to reach its potential, which its incredible demographics offer the nation? In much of our BRICs analysis out to 2050, the outlook for India seems potentially the most exciting of these emerging giants. But if India is going to get there, it is going to have to boost its productivity significantly along the way. *India Inc.* examines the key players that are shaping the India of tomorrow; these are the people that will lead the country into a new future, both in terms of what they are doing now and through the examples they set as role models."

Jim O'Neill, Head of Global Economic Research, Goldman Sachs & author of **The BRICs Report**

"One of the important trends of the first decade of the 21st century is the presence of Indian companies on the world stage. As the geo-economic weight shifts to Asia in this new century, after more than two centuries of Euro-American domination, we need to better understand the implication of the presence of Asian business leaders in the global arena. *India Inc.* will play an important role in providing a nuanced understanding of India's role in this globally shifting economic environment."

Vishakha N. Desai, President and CEO, Asia Society, US

"*India Inc.* details Vikas Pota's fascinating exploration of the business people who have provided the backbone for the past decade of extraordinary economic growth in India. Acknowledging its newfound classification as an 'emerging power' and 'land of opportunity,' Pota sets out to answer some of the more difficult questions that have arisen from this period of globalization and great success in India.

Formulating his work into a series of mini-biographies, Pota does an excellent job of addressing these questions and highlighting the traits that have allowed India's now famous innovators, entrepreneurs and legacy business owners to reach the pinnacle of success. This book is well researched, highly informative and, most of all, relevant as it sheds light on one of the world's most exciting growing economies."

Lynn Forrester de Rothschild, CEO, E.L. Rothschild LLC

"Given the heightened global attention on Indian corporate leaders, and indeed on emerging market business leaders going beyond their local markets, Vikas Pota's book is a timely look at ten Indian business leaders, each unique in his or her own way. Covering leaders across a range of businesses, backgrounds (from inheritors of family businesses to first generation entrepreneurs to professional managers), leadership styles and growth paths, the book tells fascinating stories of vision, ambition and execution."

Sonjoy Chatterjee, Executive Director, ICICI Bank, India

"Vikas Pota's detailed analysis of India's top business leaders provides comprehensive insights into the Indian way of doing business. It helps us to understand what works and what it takes to reach the pinnacle of global business."

Chandrajit Banerjee, Director General,
Confederation of Indian Industry, India

"Vikas Pota is known as a great communicator. The firm he leads shines a light on the best that India has to offer and his book goes even further, offering the scope for a detailed examination of the people behind the headlines. This book really uncovers the human side of the Indian success story – read it!"

Mark Kobayashi-Hillary, Director,
National Outsourcing Association, UK

"The story of India's outstanding entrepreneurs has captured the global imagination... and it's a story that *India Inc.* tells brilliantly. Read this book for real insight into the people and the companies that will increasingly dominate the world economy."

Rt. Hon. Patricia Hewitt MP, Chair, UK–India Business Council

"India has arrived! ... This book explores the contributions of ten of India's entrepreneurs in a way which not only answers the 'who?' but also the 'how?' and even more importantly the 'and now what?'. This book is your guide to some of those men and women who are making the difference... Enjoy your journey!"

Lord Digby Jones Kt, Former UK Trade Minister
& former Director General, Confederation of British Industry

"India's growth story has been propelled by private enterprise and the spirit of entrepreneurship. Vikas Pota appropriately indicates that the transformation is happening across different sectors. The book dives into the heart of what makes India Inc. tick. The learnings from the spectacular growth of the individuals profiled in the book are relevant for practitioners globally."

Ajit Rangnekar, Dean, Indian School of Business

"Inspiration and ideas. That's what Vikas Pota offers readers in this book that brings together the insights and experiences of some of India's most accomplished entrepreneurs. Taking a global perspective, Pota shows how these leaders are striving to solve important challenges while helping position India for international success in the decades ahead. The story is exciting and the characters are compelling –even heroic at times. Those seeking a behind-the-scenes look at the innovation that drives real entrepreneurs and fuels their success will find *India Inc.* invigorating."

Dean Dipak C. Jain, Kellogg School of Management,
Northwestern University, USA

"Everyone will be able to identify with the top ten people... Hopefully this book will encourage even more of India's talent to ask themselves 'what am I waiting for?'"

Dr Shailendra Vyakarnam, Director, Centre for Entrepreneurial
Learning, Judge Business School, University of Cambridge

"*India Inc.* is an important work for anyone who is trying to understand the India of today in the business of tomorrow. It offers a unique insight into what drives an Indian to conquer the world, to access markets beyond India and to create enduring value for consumers and stakeholders alike. This is a must-read for anyone who wishes to understand the DNA of today's Indian titans and what makes them tick around the world."

Suhel Seth, Managing Partner, Counselage, India

"Vikas Pota has been building bridges between India and the UK for many years. Now he has put his knowledge between two covers. He has done a great job showing us that India's strength is in its business leaders – their spirit, their values and their immense capacity to overcome obstacles. If you want to do business with India – read this. It will help you to understand India better."

Lord Meghnad Desai, Professor Emeritus of Economics,
London School of Economics

"An outstanding read which is both readable and informative. Unusually for this category of book it is entertaining and insightful; an absolute must-read for anyone involved with India or business or the general reader wanting to know the forces shaping our world today."

Alpesh B Patel, India Dealmaker for the UK Government and
Chairman, UK India Business Angel Network

"This is a captivating account of India's progression into a leadership position on the global economic stage, seen through the experiences of some of India's most prolific and successful business leaders. With IT entrepreneurs leading the charge, Pota documents how India's tech titans have become part and parcel of everyday lives by delivering critical services to a global customer base."

A. S. Lakshminarayanan, Vice President & Head – Europe, Tata
Consultancy Services, UK

"With TV shows about entrepreneurship like *Dragon's Den* leading our TV ratings, this book hits the mark by chronicling the success of some of India's most successful entrepreneurs. Through his interviews, Pota tells the stories of their journey to success, but more importantly asks some tough questions that provide an opportunity for them to comment on subjects such as the challenge of China, the impact of climate change, and the future of family owned businesses, which gives an invaluable insight to an international audience that debates these issues daily. A 'must buy' for anyone interested in learning what makes 'India's best' tick."

**Dr. Mohan Kaul, Director General,
Commonwealth Business Council, UK**

"Whether we're talking of how Narayana Murthy borrowed Rs 10,000 from his wife to found Infosys which today is a multi-billion dollar success, or how Kiran Mazumdar Shaw has built her biotech empire despite having been discriminated against due to her gender, or how Tulsi Tanti has stuck at it to strike it rich with Suzlon, which is his 17th consecutive entrepreneurial attempt, Vikas Pota's book is truly inspirational. India Inc. brings to the fore a new set of role models to the world, whose names will undoubtedly be taken in the same breath as Bill Gates, Richard Branson and Donald Trump in years to come. What a great book."

Bhikam C. Agarwal, Executive Vice President, Arcelor Mittal

"Vikas Pota's insights, ability to look beyond the obvious, and his outstanding ability to interpret the inner workings of the boardrooms of India's most enterprising firms makes this book an essential read for anyone interested in the meteoric rise of Indian businesses going global. If you care about the impact of some of the fastest growing global companies, then *India Inc.* is a must read."

**Dixit A. Joshi, Managing Director & Head of European & Asian
Equities, Barclays Capital plc**

Like Paris in the 1920s, which produced artists, composers, and writers who shaped the intellectual thought of that age, India over the past two decades has been prolific in spurring a star-burst of iconic business leaders that would change the course of human history. Unshackling from a command–control economy of the past sounds like such a simple idea now. But, looking back, could the future Prime Minister of India, as the then-Finance Minister of the Country – an economist by education and profession – ever have imagined that in his determination to enable India to gain access to much-needed capital, technology, and best practices when he embarked on the reform path of the early 1990s, he would simultaneously unleash a pent-up dynamism and energy of a special breed of entrepreneur that would positively influence the destiny of the 21st century? It would be from this environment of creativity and free enterprise that an indigenous but constrained private sector would finally erupt with a volcano of ideas, new business models, and vision – all imbued with a commitment to social responsibility.

The contribution of India's leadership, which persuaded a country of a billion population to open and embrace free-market principles, and then encouraged its business leaders to flourish with conscience, has now only begun to be measured as India rises to join China and the United States as the three most powerful economies on this planet. Family values, tradition, discipline, *dharma* (duty), and grit are the essential ingredients that lace together Vikas Pota's thoughtful collection of essays on the men and women who made India's transformation possible. These men and women, and this work, are a testament to democracy and to what can be achieved when imagination, properly motivated commerce, and the human spirit are set free.

Ron Somers, President, US–India Business Council

India Inc.

How India's Top Ten Entrepreneurs Are Winning Globally

Vikas Pota

NICHOLAS BREALEY
PUBLISHING

LONDON · BOSTON

In loving memory of my late father, Tansukh C. Pota.
You remain my inspiration.

First published by
Nicholas Brealey Publishing in 2010
Reprinted 2010

3–5 Spafield Street
Clerkenwell, London
EC1R 4QB
Tel: +44 (0)20 7239 0360
Fax: +44 (0)20 7239 0370

20 Park Plaza, Suite 1115A
Boston
MA 02110, USA
Tel: 888 BREALEY
Fax: (617) 523 3708

www.nicholasbrealey.com
www.indiaincthebook.com

ISBN 978-1-85788-524-8

British Library Cataloguing in Publication Data
A catalogue record for this book is available from the British Library.

Library of Congress Cataloging-in-Publication Data
Pota, Vikas.
  India, Inc. : how India's top ten entrepreneurs are winning globally /
Vikas Pota.
     p. cm.
   ISBN 978-1-85788-524-8
   1. Businesspeople–India. 2. Entrepreneurship–India. 3. Success in business–India. 4. India–Commerce. I. Title.

   HC435.3.P68 2009
   338'.04092254–dc22

                                          2009045915

Printed in India by Gopsons Papers Ltd, Noida

Contents

Introduction   1

The Compassionate Capitalist
N R Narayana Murthy
Non-Executive Chairman & Chief Mentor, Infosys Technologies,
global IT consulting giant   12

Taking on Rupert Murdoch, and Winning
Subhash Chandra
Founder, Zee TV, India's first satellite channel   36

Driving Down the Cost of AIDS Drugs
Malvinder Singh
Former CEO & Managing Director, Ranbaxy,
India's largest pharma company   54

India's Banker
K V Kamath
Chairman, ICICI Bank, India's largest private bank   76

Healing the World
Kiran Mazumdar-Shaw
Chairman, Biocon,
Asia's largest biotechnology company   98

Putting Indian IT on the World Map
Subramaniam Ramadorai
Vice-Chairman, Tata Consultancy Services (TCS),
India's largest software company   118

Mr. Bollywood
Kishore Lulla
CEO, Eros International,
India's largest distributor of films and entertainment   140

The Climate Change Billionaire
Tulsi R Tanti
Chairman, Suzlon Energy,
the world's third largest supplier of turbines for wind power   158

Right Place, Right Time
Shiv Nadar
Chairman, HCL Technologies,
India's fourth largest IT company   174

India's Mr. Manufacturing
Baba Kalyani
Chairman, Bharat Forge,
the world's second largest forgings company   192

Conclusion   209
Sources   221
Acknowledgments   223
Index   225

Introduction

A great deal has been written and said about the emergence of India as a future superpower. Its growing economic might has been the talk of countless summits and seminars in recent years as global giants and business leaders rush to get up to speed with one of the fastest-growing economies in the world.

But amid all this economic hyperbole, we seem to have lost sight of some very basic elements that define this trajectory of growth. This book was born out of an urge to dig a little deeper into the key factors behind some of the Indian business leaders who are making such an indelible mark, not just in the domestic arena but, more significantly, across the globe.

Was it a well-defined vision for the future or just a tentative inquisitiveness that led them to look beyond their own shores to carve out a niche for their businesses?

Was the "Made in India" brand crucial to their success or was it their success that actually placed the brand among some of the biggest and the best today?

Are there some uniquely Indian aspects to globalization that Indian entrepreneurs and professionals have instinctively used as the blueprint for their growth strategy?

Do they take seriously their social responsibility to ensure that India's growth does not continue to leave its masses behind? If so, does that responsibility extend to bigger-picture issues of global warming and climate change?

Are they truly winning globally, especially as the world economy contracts?

As I grappled with such questions, some monumental deals hit the headlines and offered a sneak peek into the curiously Indian brand of globalization. On January 31, 2007, Tata Steel won its bid to acquire Anglo-Dutch steel giant Corus. It redefined the business landscape as the largest Indian takeover of a foreign company, creating the world's fifth largest steel company and instantly cat-apulting Tata into the big league. The $11.3 billion deal unleashed a frenzy of interest in what Tata represented and what this would mean for jobs in Europe. My phone rang off the hook as journal-ists and analysts called to try to get some insight into an acquisi-tion that had tilted the economic balance between the developing and developed world.

I do not fancy myself as an academic or indeed a business guru who has all the answers. But as I fielded each call I realized that on this one subject I did know much more than most. Even trivia like the fact that Jamsetji Tata, founder of the Tata group, once visited Manchester to seek out new machinery for his textile busi-ness, but came away so impressed with steel and iron that he went on to establish the first steel factory in India, setting the founda-tions for Tata Steel at a time when the industrial revolution had passed India by.

The seeds of this book were sown as I recounted some of these facts to many people who were perplexed as to where this deal had sprung from. In fact, Tata's acquisition of Corus was by no means a flash in the pan but was the natural culmination of years of strategic growth at one of India's best-known conglomerates.

This got me thinking about some of the other success stories that may still be in their nascent stages but had made that all-important overture toward global markets. It was only a matter of time before more Indian names would find their rightful place in the lexicon of successful and profitable business takeovers and mergers.

Tata is now imbedded in the very fabric of world steel produc-tion. JRD's distant nephew, Ratan Tata, has successfully built on his legacy and taken his dream of being a global player to the next level, following Corus by Tata Motors' acquisition of Jaguar and Land Rover in 2008. The iconic car brands owned by the Ford Motor Company were bought for an estimated $2.3 billion, once again setting the business world abuzz with the might of this purely "Made in India" brand.

The very fact that the deal was clinched on the promise that no jobs would be lost had the unions backing the Indian takeover all the way. Of course, the global economy has been through a seismic shift since then, forcing Tata to turn at first to the British government for what can only be described as a "bailout" package, only to find the terms unreasonable. He eventually sought funds from the private sector to enable the firm to survive the worst economic crisis the world has seen since the Second World War. But this does not take away from the fact that since the buyout, Tata has stuck to its word and kept job losses to a minimum, investing all that it takes to effect a turnaround in the fortunes of the troubled European car industry.

Leaders of the Pack

The fact that the domestic Indian market is growing proves to be a major boon and safety net for Indian companies like Tata, who face the severe consequences of the slowdown in other parts of the world while their home market sees expansion.

The Confederation of Indian Industry predicts a 6.5 percent growth rate for the Indian economy in 2009–10, which is lower than its double-digit growth rates in recent years but more promising than many Western economies that are struggling under their own weight. This growth pattern has been largely responsible for the success of those Indians who have become household names through their business fervor and economic might. Many are dollar millionaires, with their every dollar chronicled by *Forbes* and *Fortune*. And though their fortunes have taken a slight dip in line with the downturn, they remain well poised for the upswing.

For me, the leader of the pack has got to be Mukesh Ambani, the older of the two siblings who each took over half of the Reliance empire after the death of Dhirubhai Ambani. Mukesh, now the richest Indian and the seventh richest man in the world with a personal wealth valued at $15.5 billion, is the Chairman and Managing Director of Reliance Industries. His empire extends from petrochemicals to textiles to oil and gas exploration. Reliance claims global leadership in its businesses, being the largest polyester yarn and fiber producer in the world and among the top five to ten producers of major petrochemical products. It exports products in excess of $20 billion to 108 countries.

If Mukesh represents "old" industry, his brother Anil Ambani is forging ahead aggressively in what is popularly referred to as the "new" services-led economy with the Anil Dhirubhai Ambani Group (ADAG). Anil's prowess lies in the fields of entertainment with Reliance Entertainment, telecommunications with Reliance Communications, and finance with Reliance Capital. He may be the younger one who has embraced new industry areas, but he has fast become the Ambani to track, following glitzy tie-ups such as the one with Hollywood filmmaker Steven Spielberg, which he hopes to leverage to take Bollywood global. He knows the subject intimately, given his marriage to a yesteryear Bollywood starlet.

While Mukesh is a reclusive and private individual, Anil is seen as flamboyant and mega ambitious – as if he needs to prove his worth. Whether it's pounding the streets of Mumbai in the marathon, or his parliamentary career, or his personal relationship with the Bachchans, the *de facto* royal family of India's much-watched film industry, Anil's businesses flourish the world over and his personality marks him out in the public eye as the Ambani to watch.

What both brothers enjoy is the head start that their father provided them, a fact that neither will deny. The true question is whether they make as big an impact as Ambani senior did by setting up a mega corporation from scratch within his lifetime.

If you're looking for an Indian business leader who's created a larger-than-life public persona, there's no beating Vijay Mallya, who enjoys the tag of India's Richard Branson. He took the reins of the United Breweries Group at a very young age and has made it a globally competitive conglomerate with business interests spanning alcoholic beverages, airlines, engineering, agriculture, and others, totaling approximately 60 companies. Among his notable achievements are the 2007 acquisition of Whyte & Mackay, one of the world's oldest Scotch whisky brands, and his genius in getting around Indian regulations on the promotion of alcohol to brand his airline Kingfisher after the beer brand he owns. His largesse extends beyond business to buying a Formula One team and holding the Bangalore franchise of the recently formed Indian Premier League, which has added to his brand recall in the hugely important Indian market.

Talking of brand recall, you just can't get away from the Bharti Airtel mobile phone brand in India that Sunil Mittal has successfully established. Known as India's poster boy for entrepreneurship, Mittal's story is compelling. At the age of 18, in 1976, he borrowed Rs 20,000 from his father to form a business that made bicycle parts for local manufacturers, which he sold in 1980. As a result of his father's position as a Member of Parliament, Mittal successfully obtained an import license in what can only be described as a closed economy. Through this, he became the sole dealer for Suzuki Motors' portable electric generators, which were imported from Japan. However, he made his name by being one of the first to identify the telecoms sector as a major growth area and subsequently lobbied to allow private-sector firms to manufacture push-button telephones in India. As India opened up its wireless telephony segment in 1995, he was one of the first to launch a mobile phone service and there's been no looking back. Today, over 5 million new mobile phones are sold every month in India and Sunil Mittal is the biggest beneficiary of this boom.

Ever keen on riding the next wave, Mittal has set his sights on the retail sector in India and has a strategic alliance with the famed US retailer Wal-Mart. Through this connection, he provides the promise of a new market in a landscape he understands all too well. So far his activities have focused on the domestic market, for understandable reasons, but given the potential of a merger between South Africa's MTN and Bharti Airtel, as India's regulatory environment changes we may see the day when a domestically focused Bharti becomes a truly global telecoms firm.

Of course, we also have to tip our hat to the other Mittal – Lakshmi N Mittal, not a relative, known equally for the dominant position he's carved out in the global steel industry. He left India decades ago to make a name for himself on foreign shores. It all started in Indonesia, where he turned around an ailing steel company and found he could apply his learning elsewhere in the world. Known for this particular ability, he charted a course that ultimately led to his company becoming the world's largest steel manufacturer by acquiring Arcelor in 2006. Now based in London, he is the richest man in the UK with billions to his name. Whether you read about his donations to the Labour Party or his daughter's lavish wedding – where it's reported he spent £20 million to mark the occasion – or buying what at the time was Britain's most expensive home in Kensington Palace Gardens, you can't but marvel at what made all of this happen.

We could also speak about the giant steps taken by the likes of Anand Mahindra, who's shaken up the US tractor market by stealing significant market share from John Deere & Co., or about his recent acquisition of Satyam Computer Services, previously embroiled in one of India's worst examples of corporate fraud.

Last but not least, we could also highlight the achievements of Kumar Mangalam Birla, who heads the Aditya Birla Group, a $29 billion conglomerate, which acquired the Canadian firm Novelis in 2007, turning the company into the world's largest aluminum producer. Among his other businesses is the world's 11th largest cement producer, the fastest-growing copper company in Asia, and the global leader in viscose staple fiber.

Beyond the Headlines

However, you won't find profiles of these high achievers in the pages that follow. The reasons are many, the most important being that multiple biographies and analyses have been devoted to them in journals and books over the years. Almost anyone with even a mild interest in the world economy is likely to have come across some of their achievements.

I felt that it was time to look at some of those who have followed in their footsteps, built on their foundations, or simply been chipping away relentlessly through the ups and downs to find themselves at the threshold of global success in their respective fields. Along with the Tatas, Reliances, and Bhartis of this world, the business leaders I describe are, collectively, responsible for putting India on the world map.

My general interest in successful people formed the crux of my inquiries when I set out to interview these high achievers, carefully whittled down to a shortlist of 10 to cover every aspect of India's growing prowess. My pursuit took me back and forth between the UK and India and across the length and breadth of India itself – Delhi, Mumbai, Pune, and Bangalore.

There is, of course, a keen focus on information technology, the bedrock of India's corporate repute and fame. The others I chose to profile present a distinctively Indian sensibility toward global expansion in fields as diverse as pharmaceuticals, biotechnology, banking, manufacturing, entertainment, and green energy.

I was curious about what each individual had done to make it into the big time. Among my themes I included questions on their early days, their perspectives on what it takes to succeed, whether their Indian heritage played any role in their thinking or business achievements, and how those who lead family-owned businesses, members of what has been termed the "lucky sperm club," view their successes in years to come.

Suffice to say that interviewing such trailblazers has been nothing but an awe-inspiring journey for me. As an entrepreneur who sees before him new opportunities and the corresponding challenges, meeting these giants and learning what they have done proved invaluable to my personal education. This experience can only be described as equivalent to studying for an MBA at a leading business school, such is the wisdom, inspiration, and practical knowledge I've gained.

The Ones to Watch

I start with Narayana Murthy because of his status as the father of Indian software. Chairman and Chief Mentor of Infosys, he is credited with creating one of the most enduring Indian success stories. Harvard Business School Professor Tarun Khanna puts it simply: "Infosys stands out on the world stage because it is possibly the most transparent and open company in the world." This worldwide respect is largely down to Murthy and his founding team, under whose leadership and guidance Infosys continues to flourish.

Subhash Chandra, the man with the Midas touch who claims he can create something out of nothing, piqued my interest simply because I had been brought up on a diet of Zee TV. My parents, like many others, saw it as a crucial link to the motherland that would balance out any corrupting influences of growing up in London. The founder of what has now become an iconic brand proved to be a man with a mission. Known as the media baron who took on Rupert Murdoch and won, Chandra's global domination in the field of entertainment remains on course. And while he may have created a name for himself in the media industry, his achievements in the global packaging industry are also nothing short of phenomenal.

Malvinder Singh offers a prime example of a family-owned business that has diversified and incorporated a world-class professional structure. Interestingly, soon after I met Malvinder he hit the economic news tickers with the sale of his majority stake in Ranbaxy to Japan's Daiichi Sankyo, and has again made news recently by resigning from Ranbaxy altogether, despite having hailed the sale as a groundbreaking "strategic deal to cement his company's future." Armed with a kitty of approximately $4 billion and with age on his side, Singh will continue to make waves. Gautam Kumra of management consultancy McKinsey speaks of his moves as "a young entrepreneur's steps towards building a global institution."

What is truly interesting about K V Kamath is the way he took a developmental finance institution and turned it into a globally recognized and integrated banking brand. Faced with the meltdown of Lehman Brothers in 2008, ICICI could have perished had it not been for the deftness, judgment, and communication skills of Kamath and his trusted lieutenants. While the heads of bank chiefs were rolling and despite the fact that he was due to retire, Kamath stepped up and offered to steer a clear course for ICICI, prior to relinquishing executive control to take on the mantle of Chairman.

While gender must not be the criterion for judging any kind of success, the fact that Kiran Mazumdar-Shaw stands out as one of India's few female entrepreneurs who started out from scratch to create a global force made her worth examining as a role model. Being a woman might have made it impossible for her to break through the male-dominated world of brewery, but that did not stop her from using her talent in fermentation to find a cure for obscure diseases in the biotechnology sector with her company Biocon. Subhanu Saxena, UK-based CEO of Swiss pharma giant Novartis, encapsulates her talent very straightforwardly: "Her combination of huge energy, passion and incredible determination gives her a fearless quality. She has shown the world what is possible in India if you put your mind to it. The sky is the limit."

In terms of rising through the ranks on the basis of sheer talent, Subramaniam Ramadorai stands out among many of his peers. He started out as a junior engineer in a fledgling Tata business, and is now responsible for propelling Tata Consultancy Services (TCS) into the big league to compete with the likes of IBM and Accenture. The company not only offers its IT expertise to help Ferrari maintain its speed supremacy in Formula 1, but has also ventured into helping aerospace companies like Boeing in their quest for efficiencies. That TCS belongs to the Tata stable is certainly a crucial factor in its global pole position.

From IT to Bollywood might seem like an odd jump, but Kishore Lulla is a very similar case study in how a relatively obscure product can become a significant tool for expansion in the right hands. Bollywood films may have been ridiculed as melodramatic and frivolous song-and-dance routines in the past, but today they command a respect that comes only when profit margins force the world to sit up and take notice. Lulla saw this potential way back in the 1970s and built Eros International into a media powerhouse ready to take on the world. I met him just as *Slumdog Millionaire* was raking it in at the box office around the globe with its typically Bollywood flavor, and it was apparent that his faith had not been misplaced. He may be my wildcard for this book, but Bollywood films have taken the "Made in India" brand to places traditional industries can only dream of.

Then there are the likes of Tulsi Tanti, a Gujarati businessman who had the foresight to realize that energy costs are crucial to the success of any manufacturing firm. What started as his need to manage his own costs soon became the solution he rolled out to his peers and to the world. Tanti sells wind turbines and can compete with Al Gore in rattling off carbon facts. His faith in wind energy, he claims, is very simply "common sense."

Shiv Nadar is another IT leader I opted to include because there is very little known about the man behind HCL. It was a proud moment for me when the company set up a call center operation in Belfast. In a single stroke, an Indian company had silenced the critics of outsourcing who dismissed it as a damaging phenomenon that was squeezing jobs away from the West. HCL not only created jobs with the new call center, but forced many of these critics to rethink their preconceived notions about outsourcing as a cheap back-end operation in developing countries. Nadar started by manufacturing hardware and has successfully made the transition to delivering high-value software consultancy services to some of the world's largest companies. Mark Kobayashi-Hillary,

Director of the National Outsourcing Association, applauds him for successfully "crossing that bridge between hardware and software to compete with the likes of Hewlett Packard as a leading service provider."

I decided to end with Baba Kalyani, the Chairman and Managing director of Bharat Forge, who took on the daunting task of changing the image of the manufacturing sector in India away from cheap, low-skill, and inferior to its Chinese neighbors by showing the world what it's possible to achieve. Take the simple fact that every second truck in the US has a part in it supplied by Kalyani's firm. Sensing the global slowdown in the auto sector, he diversified into the wind turbine business and across various sectors to expand further. Mohan Kaul, CEO of the Commonwealth Business Council, credits him with creating an enduring "brand value" for Indian manufacturing.

The Big Picture

I hope that the overarching themes of this book help create a picture of the dogged determination combined with immense self-belief that have helped many of these leaders punch way above their weight. It is important to bear in mind that most of them started out at a time when India was not today's open economy.

Until the economic liberalization of the 1990s, even acquiring a single computer meant surviving a frustrating cycle of red tape and import hurdles. Then there were the unfriendly market conditions to contend with, with many international companies refusing to do business with India because its products were synonymous with mediocrity and its government with stifling bureaucracy.

An image shift has taken decades to bear fruit and there is still some way to go. But if some of these superior brains you will read about have their way, India is well on its way to giving the world the next set of role models after Bill Gates, Richard Branson, Rupert Murdoch, and Warren Buffett.

N R Narayana Murthy

- Non-Executive Chairman and Chief Mentor of Infosys Technologies, a Bangalore-based global IT consulting giant.
- Borrowed his share of the $250 start-up fund from his wife to found Infosys with six engineers in 1981. Today, Infosys is worth billions of dollars.
- Known for his ethics and belief in good governance, and often talked about as a contender for public office. At one time his name was touted for the post of President of the Republic of India.
- A regular fixture on the Davos circuit. Infosys is one of the few Indian firms that has invested extensively in positioning during Davos in order to lead global debates on the biggest issues facing the world's largest private corporations.

The Compassionate Capitalist

A brutal encounter with Bulgarian guards transformed a young and idealistic Communist into one of the world's most successful entrepreneurs, dedicated to the pursuit of capitalism and the rewards it brings.

The event that transformed N R Narayana Murthy's beliefs was one of the first turning points in his life. It took place in 1974 in Nis, a border town between the former Yugoslavia and Bulgaria. As he described it in a speech to New York University:

"I was hitchhiking from Paris back to Mysore, India, my home town. By the time a kind driver dropped me at Nis railway station at 9 p.m. on a Saturday night, the restaurant was closed. So was the bank the next morning, and I could not eat because I had no local money. I slept on the railway platform until 8.30 p.m. in the night when the Sofia Express pulled in. The only passengers in my compartment were a girl and a boy. I struck up a conversation in French with the young girl. She talked about the travails of living in an iron curtain country, until we were roughly interrupted by some policemen who, I later gathered, were summoned by the young man, who thought we were criticizing the communist government of Bulgaria. The girl was led away; my backpack and sleeping bag were confiscated. I was dragged along the platform into a small 8×8 foot room with a cold stone floor and a hole in one corner by way of toilet facilities.

"I was held in that bitterly cold room without food or water for over 72 hours. I had lost all hope of ever seeing the outside world again, when the door opened. I was again dragged out unceremoniously, locked up in the guard's compartment on a departing freight train and told that I would be released 20 hours later upon reaching Istanbul. The guard's final words still ring in my ears: 'You are from a friendly country called India and that is why we are letting you go!'

"The journey to Istanbul was lonely, and I was starving. This long, lonely, cold journey forced me to deeply rethink my convictions about Communism. Early on a dark Thursday morning, after being hungry for 108 hours, I was purged of any last vestiges of affinity for the Left.

"I concluded that entrepreneurship, resulting in large-scale job creation, was the only viable mechanism for eradicating poverty in societies. Deep in my heart, I always thank the Bulgarian guards for transforming me from a confused Leftist into a determined, compassionate capitalist."

Inevitably, that ruthless sequence of events led to the eventual founding in 1981 of Infosys – a name synonymous with India's information technology prowess. Infosys is now the largest publicly traded software company in India and was the first Indian company to be listed on Nasdaq. Headquartered in Bangalore, it achieved the $1 billion revenue milestone within 23 years of its inception and in 2007–09 its annual revenues touched nearly $5 billion, with a market capitalization of $15–16 billion.

As the company's Chairman and Chief Mentor, Narayana Murthy has acquired cult status in India due to his dogged determination to create wealth and distribute it as equitably and widely as possible. This computer whiz tapped into the potential of IT long before many had dreamt of the impact computers were to have on our lives. As the leader of a seven-man founding team, he is credited with bringing Infosys to the forefront of the global software services and consulting business.

His company has 27 software development facilities in India, over 30 offices worldwide, including 12 proximity development centers in North America, 6 in Europe, and 9 in the Asia-Pacific region. Almost two-thirds of its business is with clients in the US, followed closely by Europe. It is now gradually focusing more and more on the newer markets of Japan, China, and the Middle East.

The key to Infosys's success remains the foresight of its chief founder, who believes that transparency and sharing wealth are vital to retaining and nurturing talent in a manpower-intensive industry such as software. He has a number of firsts to his credit, such as an employee stock option plan introduced in 1994 to attract some of the finest talent in the business. Explaining the company's ethos, he says:

"This company has been a role model for entrepreneurship in India. We have created 100,000 jobs, conducted ourselves in the right manner with all stakeholders. It is our calling to put in the best effort to ensure that this example becomes stronger and better so that more and more people can emulate it."

Global Vision

Infosys was conceptualized as an indispensable means of developing large customized or bespoke application software for corporations around the world, primarily in developed countries. As a graduate student in control theory at the Indian Institute of Technology in Kanpur way back in 1968, Murthy had a chance encounter with a famous computer scientist on sabbatical from an American university. His views on the potential of computers got the young student hooked on the subject and that marked the birth of what is today a global phenomenon.

The key to its success lies in a well-oiled and efficient "Global Delivery Model." The company was perfectly poised to spot the potential of outsourcing and leverage it to its advantage. But this is not to say that its entire strategy is pegged on low-end work executed in cheaper locations. Murthy spelt out the company's vision for the *McKinsey Quarterly*:

"We partition a large-scale software development project into two categories of tasks. The first includes those that must be done close to the customer. The second consists of tasks that can be done remotely in talent-rich, scalable, process-driven, technology-enabled development centers located in cost-competitive countries like India. The first category involves defining the project with the client and helping them install and use the software once it is developed. These activities include business consulting, IT consulting, defining requirements, installing the software, training and rapid-reaction maintenance services.

"The second category of activities includes detailed function-design tasks, detailed technical design, database design, programming, testing, creating documentation, and long-term maintenance services. We have created processes to help us seamlessly integrate the customer-side activities with those on our development side. Our model works thanks to well-developed management processes and hiring and training activities. Also, to maintain very high levels of quality, we've developed a process model that integrates the Capability Maturity Model (CMM) with ISO and Six Sigma."

It is this sound foundation based on the world's highest software certification methods such as CMM that gives Infosys the confidence to take the economic downturn in its stride. Nearly 65 percent of its revenue comes from the US, 23 percent from Europe, and 9 percent from Japan, Australia, and other countries. Plans were well underway in 2009 to expand its revenue base in Europe. It also set up a Latin American subsidiary in Monterey, Mexico, to be close to its client base in North America.

Infosys has a workforce of over 105,000 employees from 70 nationalities in over 63 countries. It is arguably one of India's most coveted employers in the IT field, bombarded with at least a million job applications every year. During 2007–08, the company recruited a record 33,177 people against its projected hiring plans for 25,000.

Unlike in the US, Infosys does not have good front-end capabilities in most European countries except the UK and certain parts of Eastern Europe. The European market, which does business in diverse languages, is a concern for most offshore IT services companies. In addition, the offshoring norms in most European nations differ from country to country due to tight regulatory norms on data security. Nevertheless, a confident Murthy says:

"Markets are rapidly globalizing with the reduction of barriers to trade. We are encouraged by the European Union's move to open up their market to the movement of natural persons by creating new visa types that will enable the freer flow of top talent.

"As corporations grow and globalize, I am convinced that the greatest challenge they will face will be the creation of a diverse workforce. We continue to hire from the best universities the world over and train them in our global education center at Mysore in Karnataka."

Infosys is famous for its Global Talent Program, focused on attracting the brightest and the best in the field from around the world. Talented young professionals are recruited from premier universities in the US, the UK, China, and Australia, among others. They are then trained at the Mysore center to create future high achievers.

The man referred to as the Bill Gates of India is still recovering from the multimillion-dollar Satyam accounting fraud, which threatened the very foundations of India's IT sector. He made an instant commitment that Infosys would not compromise on its ethics to benefit from another company's misery and chose not to poach any staff from the beleaguered IT firm.

The election rhetoric of American jobs for American people by new US President Barack Obama also forms a backdrop to Infosys's future global expansion plans. However, Murthy dismisses concern over the future of his firm's most fertile expansion ground so far:

"When you are on the road canvassing and giving speeches to win elections, you have a certain freedom for rhetoric flourish, a phrase Obama used about his own running mate Biden. That gives you an automatic flexibility, a certain freedom.

"But when you sit in the hot seat, when the buck stops at your table, you realize that you have to take very pragmatic, well thought-out, reasoned, and balanced decisions. After all, the Indian software industry is making American corporations much more efficient, much more effective, not just in the American market but in other countries too. Let's not forget it is the second largest exporter in the world.

"So while there is considerable merit in enhancing opportunities for America in the job market, the discussion has to be around how you create that opportunity. Do you remove flab from certain aspects of the operations of companies and put that money into creating new jobs for people in the US or do you want to retain that flab and create further jobs? The result will be that you are endangering the very future of those corporations.

"So I personally believe that a smarter move would be to allow corporations to become slim and trim and fit and run faster and thereby create more and more jobs for the American people. Companies like Infosys have been so critical to the success and efficiency of the operations of so many American corporations. I am confident that before taking any major decision, he [Obama] will sit down with interested parties such as American CEOs, bureaucracy, legislatures, and influential thinkers, and then come out with a very reasoned outcome."

This confidence in the American leader comes from what he believes is a shared global vision of capitalism:

"His election brings an opportunity for change. In some sense his victory is a victory of compassionate capitalism over *laissez-faire* capitalism. His victory is the victory for meritocracy among politicians because the American voters said, we care about ideas, we care about merit of the candidate, we don't care about his or her gender or race. I think that is wonderful. I look forward to some sweeping changes by him."

In this light, as the world prepares itself for the worst aftershocks of the economic downturn, Murthy continues to remain upbeat. He sees the situation as an opportunity as long as Infosys rededicates itself to the cause of global domination in the field of information technology:

"We sat down with our leaders and our mid-level managers and we talked about how this is the time when we can rededicate ourselves to our customers. We can enhance the value proposition to our customers, because once the customers see you are critical to their success and wellbeing, they will fight it out and ensure you are part of their agenda even in difficult times. It is time to become more and more essential to our customers, focus on business value and reduce cost of operations.

"We looked at the way things were going around October 2008 and came to the conclusion that we will we have to revise our guidance for the year downwards. As against a revenue growth of 19–21 percent that we had forecast, we said we will provide a new one of 13–15 percent. Clearly, the US currency had appreciated vis-à-vis the pound sterling as well as the euro and because our reporting currency on Nasdaq and outside India is US dollars, we realized it is prudent to downgrade the growth and earnings per share by 3 percent. Also, 2.36 percent of our revenue comes from the financial sector; given that this sector will be impacted seriously, we should allow for 3 percent. So we have factored in the current climate and reduced our growth rate by 30 percent. That's pretty decent."

Background

"This industry was just $150 million in 1991 in India, today it is $50 billion. We have grown by a factor of 300 percent in 17 years, which is unprecedented. Given the fact that we started this company with $250 and the fact that in the last 27 years we have grown from seven to 100,000 people, from $130,000 in 1981–82 to $5 billion in 2008 and a market capitalization of about $15–16 billion, this tells me we can indeed create large, globally respected, influential corporations from India. I am simply basing it on data."

Murthy has continued to hold data supreme from the day he started out operations from a small room in Mumbai. It remains at the core of all his concepts and decisions. According to him, if you use data to arrive at a conclusion, you avoid emotion and that in turn enhances confidence and enthusiasm. "When you look at data, you unearth patterns, paradigms, issues that you never thought possible," he stresses.

This pragmatic approach is a gift bestowed on him by his strict disciplinarian father, N Rama Rao. A government schoolteacher and later headmaster in the southern state of Karnataka, he instilled a sense of fair play in all his eight children. They moved from one small town to the other before finally settling down in Mysore. Rao was a hard taskmaster and demanded excellence; so much so that when Murthy came fourth in his entire state in some examinations, he did not receive any congratulatory rewards from his father, but a terse: "What happened to the other three ranks?" He turned to his mother, Padmavathamma, for comfort, and she assured him that it was just his father's way of making him work harder. From her he learnt the compassion that was to form the very basis of his views on capitalism:

"A couple of my father's friends would often troop in late in the evening. She invariably stretched whatever little we had, which meant that she went to bed hungry. But she never complained, there was always a smile on her face."

Growing up in a large family, Murthy recalls someone always being sick or crying. But despite the hardships, their humble household was always filled with lots of fun and jokes. They often sat around a box radio to listen to western classical music, a pastime that has survived the passage of time, with some of the melodies now stored on his iPod. His father used the example of those tunes to show how different maestros can work together to create beautiful harmonies, an important lesson that Murthy holds dear to this day; he continues to believe that "one plus one must make at least three if not eleven."

Murthy obtained a bachelor's degree in engineering from the University of Mysore, followed by an MTech from IIT, Kanpur. He started his career as a systems programmer at IIM Ahmedabad and later worked as a systems engineer for SESA in Paris. He is credited with designing and implementing India's first BASIC interpreter and time-sharing operating system. He also designed a real-time operating system for handling air cargo for Charles de Gaulle airport in Paris. He later joined Patni Computer Systems in Mumbai as the head of a software group.

It was here he met his six colleagues – Nandan Nilekani, N S Raghavan, Kris Gopalakrishnan, S D Shibulal, K Dinesh, and Ashok Arora – and they eventually created history from a tiny 10×10 foot room in the city. Each put in their share of Rs 10,000 to kickstart Infosys as a creator of quality software for global corporations. Murthy, a billionaire today, could not afford that investment and turned to his wife Sudha for the money. She could see that setting up the company had become an all-consuming passion for her husband. Though not too comfortable about giving up the security of a monthly pay check, she handed over her savings to Murthy with a clear warning that it was all they had. He said:

"My wife gave me my part of the equity in the company. It was entirely her choice. She is a better computer scientist and manager than I am. But I told her we should not mix family with business and that either she does this or I do it. She was kind enough to say I should. I took a huge cut in salary when I started. She took over all responsibilities of running the household and took care of our children very well. She encouraged every colleague and wife of every colleague and brought up two very brilliant children."

Sudha's faith proved crucial at the start in 1981. She describes herself as a clerk-cum-cook-cum-programmer while working as a senior systems analyst with the Walchand Group to supplement the household income.

The family and Infosys moved to Bangalore in 1983 to be close to its first client, MICO. They rented a small house in Jayanagar and another house as the company headquarters. Sudha held the fort while her husband spent long stints abroad, mainly convincing US companies that an Indian firm could handle large software projects. She wrote on a webpage:

"There was no car, no phone, just two kids and a bunch of us working hard, juggling our lives and having fun while Infosys was taking shape. The wives of other partners too gave unstinting support. We all knew that our men were trying to build something good."

Business

Infosys's main business is to provide information infrastructure for companies from which they can derive competitive advantage. It provides e-strategy consulting and solutions, and offers maintenance, reengineering, and enterprise integration services. It carries out large application development work as well as developing and marketing software for banking and financial services. It also establishes software centers for its customers.

The solutions the company offers cover a wide range of business areas, including e-commerce and e-business enabling, warehouse and inventory management, and customer management. About 34 percent of its revenues come from the insurance, banking, and financial sectors around the world. Recently its key focus has been to position itself as an e-consultant to move up the value chain.

It continues to compete with other Indian giants such as Wipro and recently lost out to HCL Technologies in the pursuit of Axon, a British software company that it was hoping to acquire in 2008. This would have been Infosys's largest acquisition ever and would have set it well on the course of becoming India's largest global software services provider. Nevertheless, Murthy remains upbeat about world domination:

"This is a company where people from different nationalities, races, and religious beliefs come together in an environment of intense competition with the utmost courtesy and dignity to add greater value to our customers day after day. We have achieved some success, but there is a long way to go. That to me is winning globally.

"Infosys is an enlightened democracy, a place where we argue, debate, discuss, and finally come to a conclusion based on the merit of the argument, data at hand. As Amartya Sen pointed out, democracies rarely have a crisis because the opposition makes sure the government remains on its toes. Similarly, as we are a democracy, we have not had any serious crises. Only minor ones, which are part of the game.

"As against a global average of about 65 percent of software projects being completed on time and budget, we have a record of about 92 percent of projects being completed within time and budget. That translates very clearly to bottom-line dollars.

"Similarly, because we have focused on training, and put a lot of investment into quality and productivity, the software we develop is flexible, easily adaptable, scalable, with the result that the total cost of ownership within a period of 10 years is much less in our case (30–40 percent) than it would be in any developed country. This again translates directly to the bottom line. That money could be utilized to reduce costs for the customer or create new jobs or expanding the customer base."

Infosys's biggest strength is the strong brand name it has established for itself in the IT services sector worldwide. It entered the BPO (business process outsourcing) space through Progeon, which has recently been renamed Infosys BPO. Its five other subsidiaries include businesses in Australia, China, North America, Mexico, and Sweden.

The company's strategy is to avoid being a subcontractor for large consortium-style bids or merely to provide manpower for tasks. It has clearly decided that it aims to compete for large projects that can utilize its breadth of skills. Its Chief Mentor, who is also confident that Infy is competing with the world's biggest and best such as Accenture, says:

"We are in the business of developing customized software applications to create competitive advantage. After all, strategy is all about becoming unique in a marketplace, for sustainable enhanced margins. If a corporation wants to be unique, it has to create a unique interface and business rules with customers, employees, and investors. That means you need people who can either create a customized software for you or create a customized layer around standard packages. So as long as businesses are alive, I believe we will be alive. But it is only about how smart we are in enhancing the perception of business value in the minds of our customers.

"This is the first time in the history of the world when a developing country like India has been the writer of the rules of the game. The likes of IBM and Accenture realized that to survive and succeed in the market they have to play the game our way. Are they better than Infosys? In some areas, maybe. But one thing I know: as long as we use speed, imagination, and excellence in executing everything we do, we will survive and succeed. The day we forget these three, we will disappear. There is only one insurance and that is how good we are at embracing these values."

It is these values of corporate governance and transparency that set Infosys apart from other players in the field. It was the first company in the world to publish its financial statements according to the accounting standards of the countries where it does business, including India, the US and the UK, Australia, Canada, France, Germany, and Japan. It is also credited with giving India a leading edge in the global knowledge economy and for focusing the world's attention on Bangalore as the twenty-first century's most important IT hub, dubbed India's Silicon Valley.

Turning Point

The journey to the top has not been an easy one, with a number of hurdles to overcome at a time when India was not an open economy. Simply importing a computer into the country took months. The economic reforms of the 1990s came as a blessing, but had Murthy not stood his ground, history may have relegated Infosys to the category of companies that had a brief good run. He recalls:

"There was a feeler sent to us [in 1990] that we could sell the company for $1 million approximately. After nine years of toil in the then business-unfriendly India, we were quite happy at the prospect of seeing at least some money. Five of the seven founders of Infosys met in our small office in a leafy Bangalore suburb to discuss the proposition.

"Somehow my view was that we had already run this marathon long enough, and that we had gotten used to this deprivation. I said when you have gotten used to all of this, when our wives have given up on us in terms of being successful, there is no downside. Then I said maybe we should push along a little bit more because nine years is a long time. By then, I was 44.

"I said I cannot go back and spoke about our journey from a small Mumbai apartment in 1981 that had been beset with many challenges, but also of how I believed we were at the darkest hour before the dawn. I then took an audacious step. If they were all bent upon selling the company, I said, I would buy out all my colleagues, though I did not have a cent in my pocket. Then that started them thinking that if this guy has so much confidence, maybe they also should."

That marked a crucial milestone in the company's history. The company went on to make the most of the economic reforms of 1990s India. Licensing was abolished in the IT industry, which meant not having to go to the Department of Electronics to get a license to import computers any longer. The Reserve Bank of India introduced current account convertibility, which meant that Infosys could open offices abroad, send people abroad easily, and get consultants from abroad for training in quality, marketing, and branding. Murthy explains:

"These were the few things that created a new mindset, a new paradigm and a new way of doing business. That is when we decided to go public in 1993. We raised something like Rs 13–14 crore [Rs 130–140 million] and spent part of that on building the first campus on our quality initiatives and on getting some consultants from abroad.

"We built India's first software campus and realized that because we were going public we could create stock option plans and attract good talent. That was another competitive advantage we were creating. We said we will invest very heavily in technology. Even today, I believe that we spend the highest percentage of revenue on technology of all Indian companies. So, in that sense we never turned back from that day because it allowed us to focus on the market, not worry about licensing, telephones, foreign exchange for traveling abroad, etc. In other words, all friction to business was by and large removed. It allowed us to focus on the market."

Key Strategy

The Infosys campus remains a hallmark of excellence. Several world leaders have made a special stop at the sprawling 85-acre, 49-building venue on the outskirts of Bangalore.

"When we moved to this campus, it established a new idea that software companies should have campuses in India. It would enable us to take on the IBMs of the world. Besides the opportunities for us, what happened in 1991–92 was that thanks to liberalization many foreign companies came to Bangalore. Many of my friends said, the game is up as all your people will leave and join them. We sat and debated that there were three choices before us: go to the government and get it to kick all these guys out. But that was against my principles as I have always believed in a free market. Second was to say, this is our karma, we have run the short marathon and time to give up. That was also anathema for me.

"Third, was to say let us find out what these great corporations do and let's see if we can do it even better in our own backyard. Create an excellent workplace, satisfy all hygiene conditions, green clean campus, a food court. It may be a little difficult to get to, but once there they will have a wonderful productive quality for eight hours. That proved a crucial instrument for us to win the game. At the same time we introduced stock options to ensure our people get much higher compensation than any other MNC."

The company also created the Campus Connect program, a partnership with academia to create industry-ready professionals. Murthy believes in leveraging the power of youth and is often quoted as saying, "I don't value experience as much as I value enthusiasm and learnability."

Indian Perspective

It is this faith in the youth of India that has underpinned the company's entire growth strategy over the years and Murthy's own image as an inspirational leader. This includes running a business without any gender bias and giving women an equal opportunity to climb the software chain. He says:

> "Women form 26–27 percent of our workforce. In the engineering colleges, which provide the primary source of talent for us, the percentage of women is 25–30 percent. Ideally I would like to take the recruitment of women to 50 percent and we are working towards it. We have a very good diversity program and gender preferential program. We have created various initiatives that make this a more attractive workplace for women, such as providing crèches and telecommuting for women in certain stages of their family life."

Having convinced the West that Indians could compete, he has formulated some key principles for his company based on his karmic and Gandhian beliefs: conduct a legal and ethical business; always spend less than you earn; make profits and declare dividends; and create leadership by example.

A similar value system forms the basis of his acquisitions strategy. He explains:

> "I am often asked if I have a timetable for acquisition. You don't have a timetable for falling in love with somebody. My

view is that when two companies come together they have to satisfy a few important criteria. The value system and aspirations must be very similar; they must bring sustainable complementary value to the table; there should be very little overlap of customers, to ensure scope for expansion; and a clear methodology for taking the net income percentage to the level of Infosys, which is 26 percent and the second largest in the software industry. Most others in Europe and the US are much lower than ours. It is important to see that it is possible to create a method that says in two years the composite company will not only have a greater revenue but also come up to the profit percentage of Infosys.

"It means bigger opportunities for the employees, enhanced revenues and profits, part of which goes to making the lives of our people better. It also means entering new areas of expertise, new geographies, faster promotions."

"There is of course a downside, as clearly there is a possibility of the two cultures not meshing well. The critical success factor in any acquisition is creating a harmonious environment where two cultures can come together to make one plus one 11; if not 11 at least 3. That requires an understanding of each other's cultural nuances, aspirations, and value system, and making sure that we come out with a composite aspiration and value system that ensures both parties see that they can catch a part of the rainbow and put it in their pockets.

"For the clients it means better expertise, more end-to-end solutions, better business value, and a larger portfolio of services."

All this macro-level planning is underpinned by some very simple factors. Murthy vividly recalls the sense of pride he felt on March 11, 1999 when Infosys became the first Indian company to be listed on Nasdaq. But he also fears that young people may fail to leverage all the strengths that he finds essential from an Indian perspective:

"When I sat there on the highest stool in front of hundreds of arc lights in New York City when we got listed on Nasdaq, it was a very satisfying moment. It was the first time an Indian company had got there. I used the words of Neil Armstrong, 'a small step for Nasdaq but a giant leap for Infosys and the Indians of the industry.'

"I strongly believe performance leads to recognition, leads to respect, leads to power. The best recipe that India has is performance, performance, performance. Then the world will respect India automatically. But I find around me many, many stimuli that tell me that not everybody buys into this. That upsets me a lot."

However, this has not dampened his motivation or enthusiasm for wealth creation. He believes that while around 20,000 people in Infosys have made money and improved life for their families materially, there are another 85,000 who have not had that chance. So he believes that those who have been the beneficiaries of wealth bear the responsibility to work hard and perhaps even harder to make sure that the other 85,000 derive similar benefit.

Charity

While creating this atmosphere for profit making, Murthy never forgets where these profits must go. His ethical streak comes from his parents, who believed in giving despite their poverty.

The Infosys Foundation has invested considerably in rural education, health, and infrastructure. Since its inception in 1996, it has worked to support the underprivileged. The foundation began its work in Karnataka and gradually extended its activities to other Indian states such as Tamil Nadu, Andhra Pradesh, Maharashtra, Orissa, and Punjab. It has implemented projects in four key areas of healthcare, social rehabilitation, learning and education, and art and culture. It constructed the Infosys Super Speciality

Hospital in Pune and regularly donates medicines to elderly and poor patients suffering from cancer, leprosy, and heart/kidney ailments, mental illnesses, and other major disorders. Says Murthy:

> "There are only so many houses and cars you can buy. In the end, success is when you enter a room and note the joy on the faces of the people. If their eyes light up on seeing you, that is success. And if you want that to happen, then you have to realize that the power of money is the power to give it away. A house, car, good education for your children are all important, but beyond that there are much nobler goals."

Besides his charity work, Murthy is well known for throwing his weight behind improvements to the civic infrastructure of his adopted city of Bangalore. He realized that for it to compete with the major software hubs of the world, its basic facilities must improve. He strongly believes that "improvement in infrastructure is a visible sign of progress. It's a big bonus in arguing the case for our country."

The champion of an international airport in Bangalore before a controversy forced him to resign from the project, he remains restrained in his criticism of the politicians of his state:

> "Our politicians have a very tough job. Electoral energy in India is in the rural areas, where there is not too much economic growth, where the benefits of globalization have not percolated yet. On the other hand, there is urban India where there is tremendous economic energy, benefits of globalization are happening, there is an improved quality of life for people. But unfortunately, that is only 35 percent of the country's population, while the rural folk make up 65 percent.
>
> "As a result, our politicians are in a dilemma. If they support policies to enhance the urban economy, then their rural vote goes against them. Hence they are lukewarm to the needs of urban people such as improving roads, better connectivity, power, etc. Not that they are doing anything

extraordinary for rural India, but at least they won't be seen as being partial to urban India.

"My uncharitable view is that the quality of Indian politicians leaves a lot to be desired. They are not equipped to make policy decisions in the modern world. There are a few exceptions, but a majority at the state level are far removed from what is happening in the modern world."

In light of his passion for development, there has often been discussion of him taking up political office. He dismisses talk of him being considered for the august role of President of India, as it would be too ceremonial for his *karmayogi*, action-oriented spirit. However, when asked he did not rule out an interest in becoming India's Ambassador to the US.

Murthy's vision includes making IT accessible to all and thereby reducing cost and improving productivity:

"Who wants and needs all this more than the poor? That is where compassionate capitalism comes in. It is the practice of free market philosophy with self-restraint. Many people in the world may say it doesn't work, but almost without exception, I have seen that those who want to exercise such restraint have been happy and the world has been happy with them. Others have not only been destroyed, but caused huge suffering. Enron is a perfect example.

"Living in harmony with society alongside government regulation is important. We need a good umpire, somebody to blow the whistle at the right time. But that umpire can't be playing the game or taking sides."

It is no surprise that his key role model is Mahatma Gandhi, whom he does not follow blindly but admires in most spheres of public life:

"One area where he is the supreme leader that this world has produced is how he demonstrated the power of leading by example. I am a great believer in it. In every important mission, you need tremendous sacrifice in the beginning as no one knows if there will be success. To do this, people have to trust the leader. In that sense he is the best role model."

Murthy's sense of leadership extends beyond the Infosys campus. His spartan lifestyle includes energy conservation, to the extent of rationing his daily bathwater supply. While he describes himself as a fair and ethical person, he admits to being a man in a hurry. He wants to see the India of his dreams in his lifetime:

"I am a great believer in the green initiative, in reducing the carbon footprint. I am in the middle of converting my entire house to a solar energy-powered system. I use only half a bucket of water for my bath. I realized we cannot afford a full bucket because we don't have sufficient water in the world. Before I can tell others what to do, I have to first do it myself. Then you will find that half a bucket is enough, as long as you plan it well. Time is also valuable. I write short emails and don't believe in wasting time on frivolous talk."

Future Proofing

Murthy's immaculate planning extends beyond his personal life into his business strategy. He shocked the corporate world in 2002 when he stepped down as CEO of Infosys. He handed over the reins to his second in command, Nandan Nilekani, choosing instead to be Chairman and Chief Mentor:

"When I was 52, I said we have all run this marathon together. The others too have a desire to lead this company, to leave their footprint. The best way to make it happen is to stand down and give them the opportunity. But given that I founded this business, it is very difficult to tear yourself away. Almost like separating from your daughter when she gets married and goes away. It is not easy, as she will always be your child. So I decided to find a role for myself to remain busy at a value to the company.

"I had started taking interest in outside activities and joining boards of universities etc. All my colleagues said, why don't you mentor our leaders. So as first amongst equals, I became the chief mentor for our mentoring system.

"But on June 21, 2011, I will walk out of this company. I will complete 65 years and we wrote this rule down right at the beginning. At 60, we will give up our executive responsibility and at 65, if on the board, we will leave the board.

"As to the successor, we will have to see. We have a COO. If the nominations committee finds that he is the best person, we will appoint him."

In line with his pursuit of a meaningful life beyond Infosys, Murthy has recently sold a small stake in Infosys worth approximately $37 million, to set up his own venture capital fund called Catamaran Investments, for incubating Indian start-ups and thus promoting entrepreneurship.

Family

In all of this there is no foregone conclusion about members of Murthy's family taking over the company. He is proud of the fact that both his children have grown up with a firm value system. Until her recent marriage, his daughter Akshata worked as a venture capitalist in the US after receiving an MBA from Stanford, and his son Rohan is completing a PhD in computer science from Harvard University. Murthy says:

"I have told them, it is so much more fun for them to run a new marathon of their own rather than run this one on my shoulders. And they are much smarter than I am, with a much better value system than I have. I have no doubt they will be able to do something much, much better than I have. They have a share in the company but I don't want to impose anything on them."

Meanwhile, he and his wife continue to live a simple life in the same three-bedroom house in Bangalore that they bought when they first moved to the city.

In a similar tradition to his parental home, he often comes home with unannounced guests. After the meal he does the dishes even as the discussions on data management and computer programming carry on.

"A clear conscience is the softest pillow. It is better to forgo a billion dollars than a good night's rest" is this gentle software giant's simple philosophy.

For this reason, it really comes as no surprise that Murthy was the most sought after business leader for the students of the premier MBA institution, the Indian School of Business in Hyderabad, which recently conducted a charity auction where the students had their pick of 26 CEOs that they could shadow for day. For management students and established corporate leaders alike, we're reminded by examples such as this that Murthy is in a league of his own.

Indians are used to reading about Murthy and his achievements, but others may question this philosophy, or his commitment to tackling climate change, or his simple way of living. All I can say is that you only need to meet him to know that he's on the level.

In an age of excess and über-luxury, Murthy reminds us how important it is to walk the talk.

Subhash Chandra

- Launched India's first satellite TV channel in 1992. Today, Zee is beamed into 500 million homes across 167 countries and enjoys a 26% market share of the entertainment segment in India.
- Failure to create an Indian-style Disney Park in Mumbai spurred him into taking entertainment into homes at a time when India's media airwaves were dominated by poor state-controlled broadcasting.
- Not satisfied with conquering TV, has led a strategy to diversify into film production and newspapers. *Daily News and Analysis* has displaced *The Times of India* in Mumbai within a short timespan.
- Beyond entertainment, owns a company that produces 4 out of every 10 toothpaste tubes in the world!

Taking on Rupert Murdoch, and Winning

As people of Indian origin who were born and lived outside its shores, first in Kenya and then in the UK, my parents faced a huge challenge with respect to the upbringing of me and my sister. They sat us down every day and narrated stories from epics such as the *Ramayana* or *Mahabharata*, enrolled us in clubs and classes that had any Indian connection, and in general looked for ways in which we could learn about India's languages, culture, and traditions in order to reinforce our cultural and religious identities.

When Subhash Chandra started Zee TV, it seemed that almost overnight my parents and their friends had found the ideal medium for inculcating Indian values and sensibilities through Hindi soap operas, serialization of religious dramas, news bulletins, and other such programming. Even today, if at the crack of dawn you were to walk down a residential road in Southall, home to a large number of Indians in London, and peer through each window, you'd see every household tuned into prayers at the Golden Temple in Amritsar. This, to me, demonstrates the huge role that Zee has played in the lives of those who left India decades earlier.

We hear about the genius of India's entrepreneurial business classes and Subhash Chandra typifies the confidence that's become their trademark. Famous for claiming he can create something out of nothing, the Chairman of Essel Group launched India's first satellite channel in 1992, laying the groundwork for many others to follow. What is today big business and a way of life started with this one man's vision of taking high-quality entertainment into the homes of urban and rural India.

Almost every concept in Indian television has its soul in Zee TV, be it reality shows, melodramatic television serials, or chat shows. Zee was responsible for shaping the mindset of young people starved of good entertainment and global news. The channel soon proved the perfect vehicle for the process of change and the sense of pride in being Indian that was beginning to take root in the 1990s.

Today, Zee TV maintains its position as one of the most popular Indian channels, with over 500 million viewers in 120 countries. Its reach among South Asians in every corner of the globe makes it an easy global winner. Many non-resident Indian parents and grandparents see it as the quintessential link to the motherland that will help prevent their children veering too far away from Indian values.

Being a media baron may be his biggest achievement, but Chandra is a true entrepreneur who has fingers in many lucrative pies. Starting out as a grain trader, moving on to packaging expert, and then creating India's version of Disneyland with EsselWorld, his group is valued at an estimated $100 billion, with an annual turnover of $12 billion.

Global Vision

It all began with India's bumper crop of grain in the early 1970s. Chandra realized that the Indian government would need to find effective ways of storing it. One such option was to use polythene sheets as tents. He recalls:

"While doing this, a new experiment was done with a combination of different kinds of plastic, for which we leased a lamination plant for four years to laminate one plastic with the other. That experiment didn't succeed but I had the plant so I started lamination with paper, aluminum foil, on jute and other things for packaging purposes. That's how I started supplying packaging material to pharmaceutical, fertilizer, and various other industries.

"At a packaging exhibition I attended in 1981 I picked up a lamination tube as a product and brought it to India.

That's how I entered into supplying toothpaste tubes and other cosmetic tubes across the globe. Today we have plants in all five continents. Of every 100 people who use toothpaste in the world, 37 are using our tubes."

He was astute enough to foresee that plastic would take over from metal packaging. Nevertheless, this nearly 40 percent world market share of the packaging industry did not come easy. Essel Group's offshoot, Essel Packaging, had limited capacity and was taken over by Unilever. But the latter's Indian arm, Hindustan Lever, did not use the plastic tubes for the first two years.

Being new to the trade, Essel could not push for its product nor enter the market on its own and soon began facing financial difficulties. Within three years, nearly all its capital had been wiped out. Chandra persisted and soon some local brands started using his products; in true herd mentality, others followed. Today they are so much a part of our daily lives that it is difficult to imagine a time before easy-squeeze tubes.

During the long gestation period, Chandra found himself unemployed. He decided to plow some of his profits into a piece of land lying in a Mumbai suburb and converted it into an amusement park in 1989. EsselWorld was a unique concept for India, with rides of international standard. Consumer research had suggested that nearly 3 million people would walk through the doors in the first year, but only 1 million did. Chandra concluded that while Indians were craving entertainment, they were not willing to travel miles for it.

Struck by the popularity of videos, he invested in equipping a fleet of vans that would tour the countryside charging people for watch the videos they carried. While the idea was not a resounding success, it got Chandra thinking about television. And it was while watching CNN that the idea of satellite television hit home:

"When putting up EsselWorld, I thought we were doing a good thing for the city without asking anything from the city.

But the bureaucrats and political bigwigs created a lot of problems when we set up. They wanted 150 percent entertainment tax on small ticket prices. We went through a hell of a lot of trouble. Even after we opened the park, we had anticipated 3 million guests in the first year, only 1 million came. In search of a solution to bring entertainment closer to home and make a bridge between the governed and governing people, satellite TV was the answer. I didn't know what it is, or how it works, but it took me 18 months to get it up and running."

Chandra was confident he was on to a winner with this new venture. He remembers telling a politician friend of his that he would use this channel to change the perception of India. He says:

"I told him if I am able to succeed, I could probably create at least 1 million ambassadors for the country. Those days the Indian passport was not a very welcome document. The international media would only write bad things about India, all about blood and violence in the country. No good things were shown on TV.

"I knew I could have at least 1 or 2 million homes connected outside India, out of which at least 200,000 homes would be in the Western world. With an average of five people in one family, at least 1 million ambassadors could be created instantly. If I could inform them about what is happening in India on a daily basis, I could arm them with the information they need to counter the negative image. Through a single news bulletin they would see the bigger picture. Entertainment shows would reflect how the society is really operating and chat shows would present the correct thinking process among youngsters."

A senior official at Doordarshan, India's one and only state-run terrestrial channel at the time, conducted a technoeconomic feasibility study and suggested that the best transponders for the purpose were with AsiaSat. Tracking down its CEO was a test of Chandra's persistence, but he finally got hold of him on his Christmas break in Canada in 1991. He then found out that all its transponders had been leased out to Hong Kong-based Satellite Television Asia Region (STAR). Once Chandra got the ear of the bosses in Hong Kong, they thought he wanted to sell some programming, so were surprised to learn that he wanted to start his own TV channel. They weren't convinced that an Indian company would have the money or the know-how to run such an operation.

Chandra finally reached the boardroom headed by Richard Li, son of STAR's owner and China's richest man, Li Ka Shing. He proposed a 50–50 joint venture to start a television station. But Li was adamant that it would not work in India. Chandra describes what happened:

> "I said I think there is money in India. If you don't, give me the transponder and I can run the channel. When he named a price of $5 million, there was pin-drop silence in the room as everyone present felt it was an unreasonable demand. After all, the company bought it for $1.1 million from AsiaSat. After five minutes' silence, I said OK but only if you are ready to sign today."

Still unconvinced, STAR decided to take a closer look at the Indian market. It was warned that Chandra may not be the best bet as he had no previous media experience. STAR talked to established media organizations like the Times of India and India Today, only to find that neither was willing to match the $5 million that Chandra had agreed.

Not one to give up, and sensing that other opportunities may exist, in parallel Chandra also widened his net and came close to convincing a Russian satellite company to back him. Then, out of the blue, STAR came back to the negotiating table with an offer to sell Chandra the transponder. Armed with the technology he required, Chandra launched Zee TV in October 1992.

Background

Born in Hissar, a small town in Haryana in North India, Chandra is one of seven children. He belongs to a well-off Marwari family, known for their trading skills. They settled in undivided Punjab four generations ago and entered the grain trade. By 1966, in addition to two cotton gins, they also ran a successful mill for pulses. But in 1967, Chandra's father lost heavily in cotton trading and the business's entire net worth disappeared. He was also burdened by debts to suppliers and moneylenders.

At the time, Chandra was 17 and in his first year at engineering college. His father pulled him out of university and told him that he had to find some way of helping the family business:

> "We had no capital to run any business, so I struggled to find something that we could do without putting in our money. Fortunately, I met the district manager of the Food Corporation of India (FCI), who took a liking to me and agreed to do business with us."

Learning that the Indian army was a big buyer of grains, pulses, and dry fruit, Chandra sensed a larger opportunity and found that FCI couldn't match the extraordinarily high standards required to supply the largest employer in India. Thinking laterally, he suggested that his family could upgrade the product by polishing the rice or cleaning up almonds, as a way to move up the value chain without the need to add capital costs. By doing so, he successfully turned his family's business into a profit-making entity.

Having experienced success and with a new-found confidence, his entrepreneurial journey took him further when in the 1980s, he got an added boost through the then Prime Minister, Indira Gandhi. Her Congress regime instructed the Russians, one of the biggest importers of rice, to import only from Chandra's company. Pleased with his performance year on year, he kept this preferred trader tag and made millions into the bargain.

Against such achievements, as seems par for the course in India, critics began muck raking and suggesting wrongdoing on Chandra's part. This resulted in a number of tax investigations being launched and investigated, in none of which Chandra was found guilty. Once these matters had stabilized, he turned to an age-old Marwari ritual to ensure that all future dealings were visibly above board. He described the moment as *Paani mein namak dalna*, quite literally mixing salt in water, which is as good as taking a sacred vow that would not be broken, underlining his commitment to better governance of all his multifarious activities.

Essel Packaging grew with gusto and Chandra acquired massive amounts of land, some of which was used to build an amusement park in Mumbai and a housing development on the outskirts of Delhi. Sensing the pace of growth in the capital city, Chandra identified the suburb of Gurgaon as key to its expansion and bought vast tracts of land there. Today his heaving property portfolio returns huge profits, as some of India's hottest real estate is now located in Gurgaon.

Business

Chandra's foresight in diversifying his business interests across a number of sectors has been central to his success. At the core of it lies Zee Telefilms, which began with a simple business strategy of providing cheap programming for the Indian masses. Chandra is said to have watched every single program aired in its first few years. Today, the network is distributed as far and wide as the United States, Europe, Middle East, and Africa.

Zee Cinema, the company's most popular and profitable film-based channel, soon followed. Zee Sports, Zee Café, Zee Studio, Zee Music, and Zee News were all launched, aimed at different segments of the television market.

While Hindi programs remain the channel's bread and butter, Zee has tapped into the vast potential of English-language programming. Zee Café prides itself as the first channel in India to show sitcoms simultaneously with their launch in the US.

Eyeing up a hugely important overseas market, Chandra's ambitions settled on the US and launched a 24/7 wellness and lifestyle channel called Veria to target mainstream American audiences. The multipronged project spans the TV channel, e-commerce, and retail sectors and has a five-year global rollout plan.

As proof of its global appetite, increasingly Zee content is dubbed into several languages, including Russian and Chinese. Interestingly, Chandra does not see China as a threat, but is definitely wary of its growth spree. Stressing that India needs similar political will and determination, he says:

"I respect them, they are smart business people, understand money very well. Their plans are chalked out for the next 50 years. They know what they want to do and where they want to be."

Not one to be accused of having limited vision, his ability to dream big has fueled his ambitions of transforming Zee into a global content provider. The simple reason is that with the Indian market set to become the largest pay TV market within the next decade, it's content that will count, and it's content that will earn tomorrow's dividends.

Realizing the need to move forward continuously, Chandra has always used global companies like the BBC and CNN as benchmarks. After what seemed an uphill struggle in the 1990s, today he revels in his achievements, but recognizes what is required to steal market share. He declares:

"Zee News is the largest news and regional channel network in terms of reach. We are not as big as the BBC in the news space. But we are bigger than them in terms of entertainment and languages. In that sense there is no comparison. But I know we are not doing it right, as it should be done. It will take courage. A person like me will have to intervene and say enough. Let news channels be driven by news rather than ratings and revenue. If we divorce the two, the situation can be corrected."

However, his entertainment ambition is not restricted to television. He is also credited with launching India's most successful online lottery, Playwin Infravest, which offers punters the option to punch in their lucky numbers online. Proceeds from it go into some of Chandra's charitable projects.

In 2005, he entered the unpredictable and competitive world of print media by launching *Daily News and Analysis* (*DNA*). Within the first year, the newspaper was giving the reigning Mumbai daily *Times of India* a run for its money. *DNA* is run in partnership with a well-known Indian media group, Dainik Bhaskar, which is responsible for printing and distribution, whereas editorial and marketing are handled by Zee. Signaling his opportunistic feel for the next big wave to ride, Chandra says:

"I am not just in the TV business. I am in the entertainment business. And as more opportunities come, I grab them. We are planning another edition of *DNA*, maybe in the South. I'm not a manager; I don't have the patience for it. I'm an entrepreneur."

Turning Point

You can probably imagine the energy that Chandra expends through all his businesses, and given some of the battles he's fought, it's obvious that he is fiercely protective of his many projects when faced by external threats.

The incident that gets the most attention is his dispute with global media tycoon, Rupert Murdoch, Chairman and CEO of News Corporation. Rightly so, as not many people can claim to have taken Murdoch on and emerged victorious. In 1993, just as Chandra was riding high on the success of Zee TV and planning a slew of new channels to capitalize on this new market, STAR's Hong Kong owners sold the company to Murdoch. He is believed to have signed the deal on the basis that STAR had a reach of nearly 20 million homes in Asia. It was only later that he realized that 12 million of those homes were in India and belonged to Zee and not STAR.

Given Murdoch's insatiable appetite for acquisition, he first threatened to switch the transponder off and then wanted to purchase Zee. However, Chandra was not inclined to sell. What followed was an uneasy alliance between the two, which ended in a bitter court battle. Chandra says:

"I remember telling my partners, let us move away from AsiaSat. I was confident wherever we go, all [satellite] dishes [interchangeable with customers] will move with us as we were the only game of our kind in town. But the others knew Murdoch more than I did. They were scared but I wasn't.

"They didn't support me and I didn't have the funding to move away somewhere else. I had to perforce give 50 percent equity to Murdoch as I had no choice. Subsequently, he wanted to buy me out completely, which I felt I wasn't ready to do. By now we had 30 million homes and were growing by the day. Also I had read about Mr. Murdoch's ambition to control the world's media space and arm-twist governments and prime ministers. I was determined I don't want India to be like that.

"He obviously didn't like my stand and started breaking the shareholders' agreement, which clearly prevented them from getting into Hindi programming. I had no choice but to go to court in London. His lawyers advised him that he won't win, so we bought him back. That was played up by the media as something that was never done before. Murdoch had always bought people, not the other way around."

In 1998, Zee and STAR finally settled the case. They severed all links with each other and Chandra paid £180 million for Murdoch's share of Asia Today and Siticable. Given that Murdoch had valued Asia Today at nearly £1,000 million in 1995, it looked like Chandra had won a major victory. But as part of the deal he also agreed to nullify the agreement that prevented Murdoch's new channel, STAR Plus, going into all-Hindi programming. This was to prove a big loss for Zee in the long run.

Over a decade after the deal, STAR is ahead of Zee as the No. 1 channel in India, on the strength of its Hindi programming. But what put it miles ahead of the trailblazing Zee was one game show with Bollywood superstar Amitabh Bachchan as the anchor – *Kaun Banega Crorepati?*, the Indian version of *Who Wants to Be a Millionaire?*. Despite narrowing the gap, Zee has struggled to get its pole position back and has to be content with the No. 2 spot. Chandra explains:

"We were complacent and reactive. We took our viewers for granted. When that happens, anyone can beat you. If it wasn't STAR Plus, it would have been somebody else. We are, now, moving with a focused approach and thinking. Human beings are greedy by nature and birth, otherwise the world would be a very different place. Within the next five years, we want to become the No. 1 Asian media and entertainment company – be it television, print, radio, films or live entertainment."

Key Strategy

Zee's path to the top has been carved out meticulously. Its biggest advantage is that, unlike many other Indian networks, its profits are not dependent on its flagship channel.

"We have over 20 channels and nearly all of them make good money. Zee TV only accounts for 20 percent of our revenues. I agree Zee must do better in the ratings game, but this matters less to us than it would to our competition – be it Sony or STAR."

Zee's growth trajectory reflects India's media boom. From two state-run channels 20 years ago, there is now a veritable flood of over 340 channels, and new ones are being launched on a regular basis. It is now the world's second largest TV market, with 24×7×365 programming. Zee alone has 28 domestic channels and 18 international ones and is constantly adding to its portfolio. A profitable alliance with Dubai-based Ten Sports has seen its share of sports viewership increase by 35 percent.

With Zee Cinema holding on to the No. 1 Hindi movie channel slot for years, the company has now stepped into the field of film production with a new division titled Zee Entertainment Studios, which will include Zee Motion Pictures for mainstream films and Zee Limelight for films targeted at niche audiences. Plans to launch India's first high-definition channel in both Hindi and English are currently taking shape. Says Chandra:

"With all the pillars in place in terms of captive viewership, the key to retain this audience and attract further eyeballs lies in program content. Needless to say, this has been an ongoing activity – but such is the nature of the business that it has to be a perennial activity. We simply cannot afford to take our foot off the accelerator."

Indian Perspective

With cricket virtually India's religion, it understandably attracts huge advertising revenues on primetime TV. Conscious of this lucrative opportunity, Chandra bid for the television rights for the 2003 World Cup. Although his company was the highest bidder – and therefore the *de facto* winner – the Board of Control for Cricket in India (BCCI) awarded the contract to another party. In 2006, he again bid for the ICC Cricket World Cup and once again lost for the same reason: he didn't have much experience in sports coverage.

Given his focus on creating and owning content, Chandra announced his plans to create a "rebel" league, one that was compared to that of Australian media magnate Kerry Packer, which failed. With the newly formed Indian Cricket League (ICL) creating quite a stir, the BCCI launched its own competition in the form of the Indian Premier League (IPL), which stole Chandra's thunder by becoming the official league for the 20/20 version of the game. Despite these developments, Chandra refused to give up. He explains:

"When you bid, sometimes you lose. That is the sad fact. BCCI illegally canceled the bid we had won in 2004, which was wrong. They also manipulated the legal process.

"The way I saw it they were just out to make money out of sports rather than look out for the interests of Indian sports. BCCI had taken the Indian cricket team from No. 2 in the world to the lowest level in the league tables. That was the time I said enough is enough. I will launch my own parallel team. That's when ICL was launched and the fact that BCCI launched IPL soon after proves that we were right. That was our validation.

"Our main aim was to promote new young talent in India. There is enough youth out there who are not getting a chance to play for the country. Even when they started IPL, I would not have gone ahead with ICL if they said they plan to give young new cricketers a break. Instead it focused on the same players. The youngsters were still not getting a chance. That was my dream in the first place, young players with some international cricketers thrown in as a source of inspiration and coaching."

With big money drawn in by the IPL, Chandra has differentiated his league and focused on bringing new and upcoming talent to the national stage. While not the runaway success it was intended to be, Chandra has found a position for the ICL, once again underlining his ability to find gaps in the market. Having done his patriotic duty in shaking up Indian cricket, he proudly states:

> "This country has given me everything I am today. I cannot help but be a nationalist. Zee TV was also launched with this feeling of putting India on the map and today it is."

Charity

This sense of pride in the nation is also the driving force behind Chandra's support for educational projects in India. He set up TALEEM (Transnational Alternate Learning for Emancipation and Empowerment through Multimedia) to provide access to quality education through distance and open learning. Its research arm is committed to conducting social science research in the areas of community health and communication.

Chandra is also the Chairman of the Ekal Vidyalaya Foundation of India, a movement to eradicate illiteracy from rural and tribal India. The unique concept centers around setting up small, one-teacher schools deep in the heartland of the country to educate an average of 25–30 children each.

Chandra is also trustee of the Global Vipassana Foundation, a trust set up to help people raise their spiritual quotient. Furthermore, he created the Brain Trust of India to identify and nurture gifted children. He likes to spend nearly a month away from the office every year on these various pursuits, saying:

> "It gives me another kind of satisfaction and happiness. A sense of giving back something. The joy of giving is much bigger than the joy of taking."

It is that very philosophy that guides him on other big-picture issues such as global warming. He adds:

"My belief is that as a country we are not adding to global warming. One third comes from the US alone, one fifth out of Europe. These are the high-consuming societies. Indians are still not very high consumers. I gave a speech on Capitol Hill recently where I clearly said that if you are concerned about global warming and your economy, you should give nuclear technology to India. If India starts consuming that much fuel, your Western economies will be hit for six. Fuel prices will go to $200 a barrel. It is in the interest of humanity that we use nuclear technology."

Family

If it seems as if Chandra's life is governed by work, that is exactly the way he wants it.

The white lock of hair over his right temple and his smartly tailored jackets set him apart in any media gathering. He is proud of his roots and prefers to speak Hindi as much as possible. He still enjoys an occasional *beedi*, a simple Indian cigarette made of leaf-wrapped tobacco. His friends and associates describe him as down to earth and someone who is not afraid to ask for opinions or admit to mistakes.

He has been the recipient of numerous honorary degrees, industry awards, and civic honors. He finds himself 29th in the *Forbes* list of India's richest, with a net worth of $900 million. In 1999 he was honored by Ernst & Young with the Entrepreneur of the Year Award, and chosen as the *Business Standard*'s Businessman of the Year. He was Chairman of the Confederation of Indian Industry (CII) for two consecutive years.

Two of his sons now help him with the business, but when asked about his exit strategy, he remained very tight-lipped:

"Working is my relaxation. What you enjoy doing relaxes you. I do have an exit plan, but I keep that to myself. What age I plan to retire is the biggest secret. Walking down beaten paths is for beaten men."

In many respects, Chandra is probably the most global of all my interviewees. With an impressive reach and a track record in backing new business ideas, whether in TV, film production, cricket and sports, lotteries, toothpaste tubes, and other types of packaging, Chandra symbolizes a very Indian trait – his ability to fall on his feet despite all the obstacles placed in his path.

Let's not forget that he's taken on mighty beasts like Rupert Murdoch's News Corporation; BCCI, the richest and most powerful cricketing organization in the world; and the *Times of India*, the country's biggest and most entrenched newspaper – and emerged as a winner.

Unlike his contemporaries, Chandra doesn't have an air of grandeur or sophistication. His office doesn't resemble an art gallery, his body language reflects that I'm lucky to have found a convenient time to see him, and his use of English clearly shows the lack of an international education. Despite all this, I'm willing to credit him with something that not many can claim. Through Zee, Chandra has done what he set out to achieve – he's created an invaluable bridge between the 20 million strong diaspora and their motherland, one that will prove a huge boon for India in years to come.

Chandra is so far ahead of the game that it seems naïve even to ask him whether he's winning globally!

Since my interactions with Chandra, he has let it be known that some work has commenced on arriving at a valuation of all their businesses, with the ultimate aim of formalizing the overarching understanding he has had with his brothers as to their ownership, so that each brother can have a clean break with identified ownership of a particular business at a time of their choosing. This, again, points to the clarity he possesses and his desire to be open and frank about succession issues, which have blighted some of India's most famous family businesses. We need only to look at the Ambanis, Bajajs, and their peers for the fallout that Chandra is actively trying to avoid. He says:

> "Most business families have issues, but they either do not want to face them or they don't communicate among themselves. These issues turn into minor disputes in the next generation and ultimately into big, public disputes. What my brothers and I are trying to do is pre-empt such an eventuality."

Also, at an awards ceremony in November 2009, where he received another "lifetime achievement" award, for the first time he mused:

> "I would certainly want to retire within a year or two in order to do better things than making money."

But, in typical fashion, he kept the identity of his successor close to his chest.

Malvinder Singh

- Doubled profits as CEO of Ranbaxy, India's largest pharma company, producing drugs whose patents have expired (generics) at lower cost.
- Masterminded acquisitions that brought scale to Ranbaxy and resulted in its ascent to the global top 10 generics companies, with sales of $1.7 billion and exports to 150 countries.
- Sold his family's stake for approx. $4 billion to a Japanese pharma company, thus creating the world's first "hybrid" drugs manufacturer.
- Now leads the family's businesses in healthcare and financial services as Group Chairman of Religare.
- All this before the age of 40!

Driving Down the Cost of AIDS Drugs

Malvinder Mohan Singh's dream for Ranbaxy was quite easy to paint. Whether you're suffering from a cold or a viral infection, no matter if you're in New York, Cape Town, or Jakarta, you should be able to walk into your local supermarket or pharmacy and purchase some medicines or tablets that his company produces. Sure, you can buy alternatives, but you have at least one choice that is cheaper than the others and that choice is most probably manufactured by Ranbaxy, the company that Malvinder's family took charge of in the 1960s.

It is this dream that drove everything in Malvinder's world. Not satisfied with achieving the top spot in an extremely competitive domestic market in India, on becoming CEO and Managing Director of his family firm, he set his sights on conquering the world at a time when the Indian pharmaceutical sector suffered from a very poor reputation. Malvinder made it his personal mission to turn this perception around. What is more impressive is that unlike the other business leaders covered in this book, he's only 37 years old!

There have been no shortcuts to his company's meteoric rise to become almost synonymous with generic drugs in India and around the world. Singh has worked incessantly to up Ranbaxy's game and achieve $1.7 billion in revenue, making it the only Indian company among the world's top 10 pharmaceutical giants. It has a presence in 23 of the 25 pharma markets and even sells more drugs in American supermarkets than in its home base.

Ranbaxy has sales forces in 49 countries, its drugs are sold in over 125 countries, and it has manufacturing facilities in 11 countries. Ranbaxy also has the distinction of being India's first multinational corporation due to its truly global reach.

However, the road to success has not been an easy one, with hurdles to overcome in the form of tough patent regimes and the

American stranglehold on a string of key generic patents. Ranbaxy is one of the few companies that has taken on the challenge and found the perfect formula for meeting its basic aim of providing customers with access to drugs whose patents have expired and can be produced at a lower cost by Ranbaxy.

The key strategy has been to acquire companies that strengthen its hand and at the same time to strike joint ventures with the world's major firms, combined with conducting research and development to discover new drugs – a departure from the norm, as the generics industry revolves around exploiting drugs that already exist. Singh explains:

> "Our aim is very simply to help people get cheaper medicines. Ranbaxy is here to ensure access to high-quality generic drugs at an affordable price."

And the company's motto of "Trusted Medicines for Better Lives" encapsulates just that ambition.

Global Vision

It was the vision of his father, Dr. Parvinder Singh, to create a global business that resulted in Malvinder following in his footsteps and turning this dream into reality. In 1993, probably for the first time, Ranbaxy laid its cards on the table by stating that it aspired to become a research-based international business, thus signaling its intent to develop its own drugs. More importantly, its mission extended beyond simply being an exporter of products to establishing the company's presence in different regions. Singh says:

> "It is that mission statement that will take us through many, many years. That really has been the guide for me. It was my father's vision to go beyond Indian shores and become a global leader. Being international is not about being an

exporter but localizing your presence and having local people run that and gain leadership position in key markets."

Operations in the US began with the setting up of Ranbaxy Pharmaceuticals Inc. as a wholly owned subsidiary. A major milestone for the company came in 1992, when it reached a marketing agreement with American pharma giant Eli Lilly & Co.

Having been impressed with Ranbaxy's ability to resynthesize and compete in the generics market once its own anti-infection blockbuster drug, Cefaclor, was out of patent, Eli Lilly set up a joint venture in India to produce and market its branded pharmaceuticals for the domestic market. At the same time, Lilly agreed to market Ranbaxy's generic medications in the United States. Through this Ranbaxy gained wide-scale access, backed by a highly respected company, to the world's single largest drugs market.

Ranbaxy established a subsidiary in Raleigh, North Carolina. In 1995, it stepped up its US presence with the purchase of New Jersey-based Ohm Laboratories, which provided Ranbaxy's first manufacturing plant in that market. Construction of a new state-of-the-art manufacturing wing then also began, a facility that enabled the company to expand across the United States. In 1998 it began marketing its generic products under its own brand name, followed by the launch of its marketing operations in Brazil, which proved to be a cornerstone in its strategy to expand throughout the Latin American market.

Ranbaxy also expanded in Europe, with a subsidiary in London and an agreement in 2000 to acquire Bayer's Germany-based generics business, Basics. It also added production plants in Malaysia and Thailand.

By then, Ranbaxy was well on the path to global domination, with nearly 80 percent of its sales coming from outside India and overseas revenue consistently contributing around two-thirds of its turnover.

Singh was incessant in his pursuit of foreign companies. Among his foreign acquisitions were the unbranded generic drugs business of Allen SpA (a division of GlaxoSmithKline) in Italy; Terapia in Romania; Ethimed, a generics company in Belgium; the Mundogen generics business of GSK in Spain; and Be-Tabs Pharma in South Africa.

He has also taken over or acquired strategic stakes in a host of Indian companies such as Zenotech Laboratories, Cardinal Drugs, Krebs Biochemicals, and Jupiter Biosciences. Quite recently he was involved in a raid on the Chennai-based Orchid Chemicals. He picked up a 15 percent stake in the firm and denied this was a hostile takeover, explaining:

> "We are clearly in a very strong trajectory of growth. We will continue to leverage our organic and inorganic alliances as a model for growth. Our industry is consolidated globally and there are huge opportunities in the generic space. Life expectancy will continue to be on the rise and the huge healthcare cost pressures in the developed world will mean a greater shift towards generics. We are well positioned to take advantage of that expanding market.
>
> "We are there in every developed and emerging market, we just need to go deeper. I see us in the next five years continuing to grow at a 20 percent growth rate, hitting our $5 billion target by 2012 and being in the top five generic companies globally. As we move towards that, we plan to continue making significant investments into intellectual property creation for new chemical entities (NCE) and drug delivery systems."

Ranbaxy's global edge also comes from its strong focus on R&D, which employs nearly 1,200 scientists and attracts investment of nearly 5 percent of its turnover. The areas of interest include urology, asthma, and anti-bacterial segments. Ranbaxy became the first Indian company to receive royalties for an out-licensed research product – Cipro-XR, a one-a-day version of the anti-infective Ciprofloxacin licensed to Bayer and launched in the US market.

The company proved its skills in new chemical entity research by out-licensing its molecule for the treatment of benign prostatic hyperblasia to Schwarz Pharma in 2002.

Singh has a clear plan:

"For me, living in the global village like we do today, it's a very different world from what it was five years ago. What I'm doing is really reinventing the company to keep it successful and moving forward. On the one hand, we have reconfigured the business in terms of countries. Today we have a much bigger balance between developed and emerging markets.

On the other hand, we will continue to expand our therapeutic portfolio to get into more niche areas. These will be specialized products with strong profit margins but big risks too. All this will be done through a combination of acquisitions, alliances, and in-house capabilities."

One of the most significant alliances came in the form of his audacious plan to sell off his family stake in Ranbaxy to Japanese firm Daiichi Sankyo in 2008. The $4.6 billion deal instantly catapulted Ranbaxy from 22nd in the global pharma sector to 15th. The combined company is worth about $30 billion and Singh took charge as Chairman of this expanded entity. When quizzed about whether the move to sell 34.8 percent of his company was akin to selling off the family silver, he declared:

"When you are the leader, you have to set the pace for the industry... [This] puts us on a new and much stronger platform to harness our capabilities in drug development, manufacturing and global reach. Together with our pool of scientific, technical and managerial resources and talent, we will enter a new orbit to chart a higher trajectory of sustainable growth... in the developed and emerging markets, organically and inorganically. This is a significant milestone in our mission of becoming a research-based international pharma-ceutical company."

Nevertheless, many experts and peers could not help but feel a tinge of regret that a major, successful company that had become part of the Indian psyche was about to be reduced to a subsidiary of a semi-successful Japanese firm at the bottom end of the top 20. Daiichi Sankyo President and CEO, Takashi Shoda, tried to be reassuring:

> "While both companies will closely cooperate to explore how to fully optimize our growth opportunities, we will respect Ranbaxy's autonomy as a standalone company as well."

The result is a mutually complementary hybrid business model that dramatically enhances Ranbaxy's ability to pursue business development in emerging economies, and extends its reach to include both proprietary and non-proprietary drugs. It also reduces the risks in an increasingly uncertain market.

The main benefits for Daiichi Sankyo from the merger are believed to be Ranbaxy's low-cost manufacturing infrastructure, supply chain strengths, and access to emerging markets. Ranbaxy, on the other hand, gains access to Daiichi Sankyo's research and development expertise to advance its branded drugs business. It also gains easier access to the much-coveted and nascent Japanese generics market.

Prior to the deal being made public in 2008, the market was rife with rumors about Cipla, another Indian generics company, being gobbled up by a global pharma major. It came as a total surprise to the industry when it was in fact Ranbaxy that announced its sale. What added to the unexpectedness of the move was that a few weeks earlier, Malvinder had insisted that Ranbaxy, under its own steam, was considering major acquisitions to bolster its position.

While his tenure with the new entity was contracted for five years, Singh announced his resignation in May 2009. His stepping down should come as no surprise given that Ranbaxy had announced a full-year loss and the share price had tanked. Nevertheless, the decision to relinquish executive charge is said to have been on amicable grounds, and the Japanese owners were grateful for the Singh family's contribution.

Background

Born in 1972 to Dr. Parvinder and Nimmi Singh, even in his formative years Malvinder demonstrated an enormous appetite for success. Despite having what could be interpreted as an extremely privileged childhood – with schooling at India's leading academic institutions like Doon School in Dehradun and St. Stephens College in Delhi, where he read Economics – he showed the same drive to better himself as can be seen in his professional career.

Soon after graduating, not one to sit idle and live the life of a rich playboy, Singh began mapping out his career by joining American Express Bank in Delhi in 1993. While he could have pulled strings to ensure a good job, he started at the bottom of the ladder and gather hands-on experience right through from the teller counter to other departments.

He demonstrated the same enthusiasm when he decided to join the family firm in 1994. He started as a management trainee and began sharpening his sales and marketing skills. Not one to shirk hard work, he then took on a challenging role as a sales rep that brought him into contact with doctors and those who bought his company's products, the net result being that he was able to understand what customers wanted and, more importantly, gain their thoughts on what could be done better.

Ranbaxy Laboratories had its origins in the early 1960s when Ranjit Singh and Gurbux Singh, two employees of a Japanese pharmaceutical company operating in India, formed a pharmaceutical preparations company in Amritsar, Punjab. The two merged their names to come up with the name for their company. After nearly 50 years, the company seems to have come full circle with its new-found home in Daiichi Sankyo.

Like many Indian drug companies of that era, Ranbaxy linked up with a European pharmaceutical company and began production in 1962. The owners sought additional financing and turned to local moneylender Bhai Mohan Singh, a native of Pakistan who had arrived in India at the beginning of the decade. By 1966, the pair had built up debts to Singh of more than $100,000. When he came to collect, the Ranbaxy partners offered to turn their company over to him instead.

Bhai Mohan Singh agreed to the deal and began to build one of India's largest business empires. Ranbaxy initially maintained its strategy of preparing and packaging existing branded pharmaceutical products for the Indian market. The entry of Singh's eldest son, Parvinder (Malvinder's father), to the company in 1967, however, marked the firm's true modernization.

As a result of the new experiences and exposure he gained while studying for a PhD in Chemistry at the University of Michigan, Dr. Parvinder Singh was able to dream that little bit bigger than his father. During his initial period at Ranbaxy, the firm's fortunes took a positive turn in 1970, when the Indian government passed legislation that effectively ended patent protection in the pharmaceutical industry. Indian pharma manufacturers were now able to produce low-cost, generic versions of popular yet expensive drugs, revolutionizing the drug industry. The Singhs quickly took advantage of India's large, highly trained, and relatively inexpensive workforce, building up a strong staff of chemists and chemical engineers to reverse engineer drugs from the developed world.

In 1969 it launched Calmpose, a generic formulation of the hugely popular Roche discovery Valium that immediately placed Ranbaxy on India's pharmaceutical map. The company expanded quickly, and by 1973 had opened a new factory in Mohali, Haryana, for the production of active principal ingredients (APIs). To finance its growth, the company listed on the Indian stock exchange in the same year.

However, around the same time Ranbaxy also hit the headlines over a number of family wrangles. As the company expanded, Bhai Mohan Singh involved his other sons Manjit and Analjit in the business. This family affair caused tensions and in 1989 he split his empire three ways between the three brothers. There were also differences over the company's expansion and professionalization strategy, and in a 1999 boardroom coup of sorts, Bhai Mohan Singh was forced to bow out, souring his relationship with his eldest son Parvinder.

Controversies continued to dog the family after Bhai Mohan Singh's death, with Analjit Singh claiming Ranbaxy shares for the Bhai Mohan Singh Foundation. His brother Manjit challenged the very authenticity of Bhai Mohan Singh's will, triggering a family feud that dominated Indian business for years. Things became even uglier when Malvinder's mother, Nimmi Singh, charged Analjit Singh with assault. The family was eventually able to reach an out-of-court settlement in 2006.

Nevertheless, through all the difficult times and despite the challenges Parvinder faced, his influence on his son remained and their strong relationship flourished for the next three years, during Malvinder's apprenticeship at Ranbaxy.

Realizing his need to pursue further education, Malvinder enrolled for an MBA at the renowned Fuqua School of Business at Duke University in the US. It was during that time that he opted for a summer job at Merrill Lynch in Singapore, a market in India's backyard to which he had had no real exposure but that was gaining credibility as an emerging powerhouse. He spent two or three months of summer training immersing himself in the minutiae of deal making and corporate finance across a number of industry sectors, experience that can only have benefited him at Ranbaxy. He recalls:

"I would work 90–100 hours a week. I really slogged and the learning experience was incredible. By the time I came back to India, I knew all the markets well."

It was during this period that the family learnt that Parvinder Singh had contracted cancer. This triggered Malvinder's return to India to be at his father's side and to shoulder his family responsibilities in his capacity as the eldest son.

Business

Armed with valuable real-life corporate experience in Singapore, in 1998 Malvinder joined Ranbaxy's corporate finance department. A few days before his father passed away in 1999, he was promoted to become an integral part of the firm's strategy team, with responsibility for marketing. In this role he sought to put his own stamp on the firm by adopting a focus on the rural marketing division, as he realized that the vast majority of Indians live in rural areas and presented an untapped opportunity.

He also brought together a new division called Rextar for the IT-enabled market. Through Rextar, Ranbaxy became the first pharmaceutical company to have an interactive website for doctors and patients and entered the *Limca Book of Records*, the Indian version of the *Guinness Book of Records*, for being the first to offer a direct doc-to-doc chat. The idea behind the IT-enabled services was to provide access to medical data and facilitate convenient decision making. Malvinder oversaw the activity until 2000 when it was time for him to shine as Director, Global Business Development.

With Ranbaxy on the ascent in international markets, Malvinder sought to move Ranbaxy up the value chain by adopting a different approach to drug development, in the context of heated debates on the role of the licensing (of patents) in the future of the pharma industry. He continually demonstrated that he had a firm grasp on the future of the business, saying:

"Business is in my blood. I come from a business family and am a natural entrepreneur. I am very clear about where the business is at, its strengths and weaknesses. I started out as a management trainee. I was given some very challenging assignments at a very young age. With the kind of team I had, I was able to make a success of it. The advantage is I have rolled up my sleeves, seen the pain, gone through it and know exactly how to move forward. And that is done collectively as a team. I am fortunate to be surrounded by some very competent people."

One of the things that marked his father, Parvinder Singh, out from the rest of the pack was his commitment to adopting a different approach. At a time when the boards of India's biggest firms were packed with the founder's relatives, he assembled an impressive team of outsiders who were entrusted to take the business from strength to strength. For this reason, it came as no surprise that his lieutenant and no. 2, D S Brar, was installed as Managing Director after his death. A friend and former bureaucrat, Tejender Khanna, became Chairman. While Ranbaxy was known to be wedded to the principle of meritocracy, it came as a surprise that on Brar's retirement it promoted a non-Indian, Dr. Brian Tempest, to the role of CEO, with Malvinder and his younger brother Shivinder exercising their roles as the largest shareholders in the business.

However, the brothers soon took control of the firm to fulfill their own vision. Malvinder's father-in-law, Harpal Singh, was appointed Chairman and Malvinder himself took over as CEO. Tempest became Chief Mentor, a title that gained popularity when Narayana Murthy of Infosys adopted the role. With Malvinder in the hot seat and his father-in-law to provide cover, there was no doubt that the firm was back in the family's control. This seemed to be a retrograde step for a company that flaunted its "professional" set-up. Singh explained at the time:

"Family-owned businesses in India are in a completely different world today, a lot more professional. Ranbaxy has always been professionally run. It may be a family business but we are in the midst of transforming it into a completely different entity. The figures speak for themselves: profits have more than doubled since I took over as CEO and the growth prospects are much better."

Turning Point

Once Malvinder Singh was at the helm of the empire, some tough decisions were inevitable. Along with his younger brother, he agreed that the company would focus entirely on healthcare. Ranbaxy divided the globe into four regions from a management perspective, comprising Europe, Africa, and the Commonwealth of Independent States as one region; Asia-Pacific as the second; America as the third; and India and the Middle East as the fourth. A global marketing team was created to provide support to the four regions, employing over 12,000 people across the world. It also has the largest salesforce among all pharmaceutical companies in India and makes significant investments in R&D.

Singh realized that speed was a key factor in staying ahead of the pack and therefore made sure it was able to work backwards, from when a patent expires to when a new drug is on the supermarket shelf. Despite becoming embroiled with US and other authorities about alleged breaches of patents, in which some court cases have been won and others lost, Ranbaxy continues to pursue an aggressive strategy of developing generics, often referred to as "copycat" drugs.

In one noted battle, it took on American drug maker Pfizer over its patent in 17 countries for the cholesterol-lowering drug Lipitor. In 2007 Pfizer lost out to Ranbaxy in its bid to extend the patent until 2011. Malvinder declared:

"Ultimately we were able to bring forward the launch of our drug by a few years. That is the strategy we will carry on with, to keep launching products as we keep winning in different markets. Our manufacturing and R&D teams, centralized in India, are networked with the business division to work as a team, taking decisions on what products to make, how to prioritize the products and fix the target dates to launch in the market. They work backwards to see how quickly and efficiently we can take products to the market. We launch two to three products every day around the world – that's over 1,000 products a year. America is the mother of all markets and we have succeeded in shaving 15 months off the patent life of some products."

The company worked on a dual strategy of beating branded generic products in its own markets and in the longer term getting R&D pipelines in place to launch new products. As Singh said:

"Over the years, we have got our timing just right. We are the clear market leaders in India and the most respected company, be it with doctors or patients. We are also the preferred partners for people coming in. We are way ahead because we thought out of the box, not only entered but created markets for others. At a time when everyone was looking at the domestic market, we were looking outside. We started our internationalization way back in the 1970s with a joint venture in Nigeria.

"India was very inward looking back then with strict licensing systems. Ranbaxy went out and evolved and delivered. No one knew of India as producers of quality pharmaceuticals. As we delivered consistently, others had it much easier because they were seen as coming from where Ranbaxy came from. But we still managed to keep up our head start and remain ahead of the game."

The merger with Daiichi Sankyo was part of a plan to maintain that lead. Like every good leader, Singh could foresee problems ahead had Ranbaxy chosen to continue alone.

Three factors weighed heavily in Singh's decision to unlock the value that had been created. While the company had thrived on selling off-patent drugs in the US, the simple fact was that the costs being incurred by fighting these mammoth battles were ballooning and therefore making the generics market a very expensive proposition. In addition, competition was becoming fiercer and, with technological progress, the barriers to entry were also lowering. Finally, with the Indian government's love of continually extending its regime of price controls, the domestic pharma industry had been finding it difficult to generate profits.

At the time, Singh defended his decision to sell by explaining:

"Ownership does not make any difference to me. I am here to fulfill my dreams and the path I have chosen now is to help me achieve this better."

And in fact, the "strategic deal" does seem to have paid off for the family, simply because Singh sold before the stock market went into freefall. It had taken huge strides by signing an exclusivity contract on a drug with Astra Zeneca and had a war chest to invest in its development, which ensured that Singh secured a healthy premium on his shares.

The story for Daiichi Sankyo, which saw this as a groundbreaking deal, could not be more different. It has been saddled with a full-year loss from Ranbaxy coupled with a full-on fight with the US Federal Drug Administration, which went to court to force Singh to cooperate on various investigations that have since been widened to include several contentious issues such as falsifying data and manufacturing quality problems.

Throughout this saga, Singh demonstrated his ability to read the writing on the wall and bow out at the right time.

Key Strategy

It is this aggressive leadership style that sets Singh apart from some of his peers. He has never flinched from taking risks and continues to do so. Admitting to an insatiable appetite for growth, he said:

> "Not taking a risk is the biggest risk you can take. In today's world as a businessman you have to take some risks. Of course, you have to be calculating and read the market right. I have got it wrong at times, felt the pain but then moved on. It has spurred me to restructure the company internally to make it more agile and flexible. If a company is successful, you tend to be that much more blinkered about failure. Today we have a team in place which is far more effective in resolving hurdles."

Singh and his younger brother Shivinder, also a Duke University alumnus who is in charge of Fortis Healthcare, have embarked on a journey to create an integrated healthcare delivery company by investing some of the funds they've unlocked from the sale of Ranbaxy.

With this huge war chest, the brothers have upped the number of hospitals they own from 28 in 2008 to 40 in 2009, with their acquisition of rival healthcare firm Wockhardt's portfolio of state-of-the-art hospitals, and refuse to put a figure on the ideal number of hospitals they intend on managing. To use words that Malvinder Singh would probably craft in his ambitious style, "Why limit your ambitions?"

Singh shows no sign of letting up and talks of aggressive growth, especially as there is a massive gap in the demand and supply of healthcare services in the Indian marketplace. Often linked to international deals, he's made it abundantly clear that India presents the biggest opportunity for Fortis in the next period of its growth.

Through Fortis Healthcare, they are also stepping into the field of medical education and will create 10 medi-cities over the years with an approximate investment of $500 million. As a result of their patient-centric model, they hope to tap into the medical tourism market, where patients from across the world admit themselves to their hospitals for the most minor through to the most challenging types of operations on the basis of a competitive cost structure.

Singh also launched Religare, one of the fastest-growing and most diversified non-banking financial services companies, which presents itself as the "investment gateway of India." With acquisitions such as one of London's oldest brokerage and investment firms, Hitchens, Harrison & Co., it acquired global scale to complement its reach in 490 cities and towns across India. With a view to delivering globally benchmarked products and services, Singh struck deals and established partnerships with globally renowned firms like Aegon for life insurance, or Macquarie of Australia for its wealth management business.

Since his departure from Ranbaxy, Singh has spoken of the need to grow these businesses and evaluate new opportunities on a global scale. While he's otherwise been tight-lipped, one can only assume that by appointing professional CEOs for these two companies, he has given a clear indication that he intends to look at strategic growth options rather than getting bogged down in the minutiae of running Fortis and Religare. He stresses:

> "There are three very clear things I know are a must for the growth of this business – it is of absolute importance for us to be the market leaders, to create centers of excellence and run them with a clear set of values."

Indian Perspective

It was this ability to keep his eye on the ball that led Singh into emerging markets. Nearly 55 percent of Ranbaxy's business was located in new markets and its focus was on creating a core infrastructure in the region. The path of this aggressive expansion was made smooth simply because the driving force behind it all brought with him a unique Indian sensibility. As Ranbaxy gobbled up companies in different corners of the world through cross-border M&A deals, his ability to recognize where he could make the vital difference ensured the success of each entity after its integration into the Ranbaxy powerhouse. Singh said:

> "We are a global company that happens to be headquartered in India. India is one of our markets and the hub for our R&D and a substantial part of our manufacturing. But we are manufacturing in 11 countries and we have over 50 nationalities working for us. Whether we acquire a company in India or abroad, I will have a global team working on it. But at the same time, I take a great deal of pride in having my origins in India. My business thinking is global but my values and my roots are in India."

Singh was determined that Ranbaxy would come to signify all that is good about India's growth and expansion drive. Besides sheer aggression in acquiring international companies, Singh was instrumental in developing a brand of integration that gives his companies a distinctive edge in the global marketplace. The picture on his desk of him with US Secretary of State Hillary Clinton is a constant reminder of his high-flying life and global ambitions. He says:

> "It is up to the Indian companies to demonstrate their good intent. A lot of times when new companies move into a new space, there is a lot of uncertainty around cultural issues and the future. It is inevitable that businesses will change hands and we will see emerging countries play a far greater role in shaping businesses and creating global organizations. While that is happening, India must be seen as coming in as

collaborators and true partners, yet creating new synergies and adding value. It is important to build that comfort level and remove any ghost from people's mind."

Singh is well equipped to create that comfort level with all his acquisitions. He has acquired over a dozen companies and has been successful in integrating them seamlessly into the main business. As proof of his skill, recently another major Indian generics company, Dr Reddy's Laboratories, announced its exit from all but 15 of the 40 markets where it was selling low-cost, generic medicines, which reports suggest was as a result of problems in turning around companies that it had acquired in places like Germany. Singh comments:

"When we acquired the largest independent generic company in Romania some time ago, there was a fair amount of uncertainty. We merged our Romanian business with the new acquisition, created a joint brand Terapia Ranbaxy, picked a manager from that team and put him in charge as Country Manager. The message that went out loud and clear was that whoever is most competent and capable will run things.

"While we acquired them, we were the ones to merge our business into theirs. That spoke volumes in terms of our intent and what we wanted to do. We didn't move any manufacturing to India, in fact we doubled our workforce in Romania and made investments to upgrade their facilities. The whole atmosphere became positive whereby they were happy to be bought over."

And he has similar words of advice for companies coming into India:

"Be patient. India is a huge market but you will have to go through the initial pains. The results in the end will be well worth it."

Charity

This Indian sensibility stretches beyond the business to his corporate social responsibility. Ranbaxy hit the headlines in 2003 when former US President Bill Clinton used the company's R&D facility in Delhi to launch his foundation to facilitate access to cheap medicine in the developing world. Ranbaxy committed to reducing the cost of HIV/AIDS drugs and helped bring that down from around $20,000 to $80 a year.

It completed phase 2 clinical trials on a non-chemical entity for malaria, which is not aimed at boosting profit margins but at combating disease in the developing world. Singh explained:

"We come from an emerging market and our commitment is to help people use our skills and scientific know-how and acquire drugs at very, very affordable prices. In India, Ranbaxy is actively engaged in remote villages through medical vans and preventive education. These have shown remarkable improvement in certain health indices."

This enthusiasm extends to big-picture issues like climate change. Ranbaxy is a frontrunner at putting non-polluting technologies in place at its plants and ensuring proper recycling of waste. As a result, it is one of the few Indian companies that earns carbon credits.

China

Unlike many other Indian companies, Ranbaxy never saw China as a threat but more as a market. It was one of the first to set up a joint venture back in 1993, facilitating its entry into that market with a production facility in Guangzhou. Singh said:

"China is a very good and challenging pharma market. We see it as a big opportunity and source a lot of products as raw materials from the region. There is obviously competition but we see ourselves more as partners."

The company's presence in Japan was on a similar footing, despite it being one of the toughest markets in the world with extremely high entry barriers. Of course, since the acquisition by Daiichi Sankyo it has the inside track.

Future Proofing

Its reach across the world prevented Ranbaxy from relying too heavily on any particular area. The US remains its biggest market, but there is enough of a spread across emerging markets to balance out any possibility of economic dependence on the global giant. Singh said:

> "It is crucial to work with customer needs. Our strength lies in being vertically integrated. We align with companies at different ends of the value chain to be faster, service customers better, and be more cost effective. Our key is that as an organization we have been far more adaptable. We have learnt to live with change and uncertainty. In fact we are very comfortable with it."

Family

However, all of this has come at a price. For example, Singh grudgingly admits to never switching off his BlackBerry. When he does eke out some time to spend with his wife and three children deep in the countryside or on a family vacation in Singapore, he has his finger on the pulse of his corporation every second of the day. In fact, when asked what he was going to do after he resigned from the Ranbaxy board, he responded by saying he was planning to take a long holiday!

His love for photography usually takes a back seat and he is hardly even able to find time to catch a film starring his favorite Bollywood actor, Amitabh Bachchan.

He loves to drive around with his family at the weekends, despite the craziness of the traffic in Delhi. And his emotional side is evident from his choice of car, a Mercedes that belonged to his father Parvinder and will most likely remain in the family and be passed on to the next generation.

What I found most remarkable during my time with Malvinder Singh was not only his ability to focus on his achievements, but his pragmatic enthusiasm and drive to ensure that Ranbaxy's longer-term future was secure, by selling his stake to a major-league firm.

He is sometimes construed as aggressive, and I was clear during my interview that this wasn't someone I'd want to pick a fight with. Whether it was the thorough bag search when I entered his office or how he sat, ready to pounce, or even his emphasis on certain words, I walked away thinking that he could be ruthless in business. To my mind it's quite simple: he's hungry for action and he's going to throw everything at achieving his dreams.

While Malvinder Singh may not have founded Ranbaxy, there is no doubt that he took the company to a wholly different level by adopting strategies and practices that are internationally recognized. He's been accused of many things – from ripping off the big pharma companies in order to develop and market his drugs right through to selling the family silver to a foreign entity – but more important is that despite all these issues, everyone wants to do business with him. You can't take away from the fact that he's done it his way and has landed on top.

Singh is clearly winning globally and be assured, he will win in whatever game he chooses to play.

K V Kamath

- Chairman of ICICI Bank, India's largest private bank with a global footprint.
- Total assets of $102 billion, 25 million customers worldwide, 1,520 branches around the world.
- Saw the potential of leveraging technology to provide global market advantage.
- President of the Confederation of Indian Industry (2008–09).
- Awarded the Padma Bhushan, one of India's highest honors, by the President of India in 2008. Also conferred with the "lifetime achievement award" by the *Financial Express* Best Bank Awards and the NDTV Profit Business Leadership Awards in 2008.
- On retirement as MD and CEO of ICICI, was appointed Non-Executive Director of Infosys Technologies, reaffirming his understanding of and passion for technology.

India's Banker

It may be easy to coin phrases, but to embody them in reality is the sign of a true leader. Kundapur Vaman Kamath certainly falls into that category. He not only came up with the adage "bias for action," but has shown how it works on a day-to-day basis at every level of the banking world.

The former MD and CEO of the Industrial Credit and Investment Corporation of India, more popularly known by its abbreviation ICICI, has dominated world business headlines for achieving one of the quickest and most audacious turnarounds in a company's fortunes, making it India's largest private bank in terms of market capitalization. With assets of over $100 billion, the country's second largest bank after the government-owned State Bank of India serves a vast global customer base via more than 1,520 branches and 4,485 cash machines across 18 countries.

The key to this rapid and sustained growth model has been the vision of K V Kamath, who was convinced that ICICI's competitive edge would come from the use of technology. This was at a time when none of the other Indian banks had begun exploring the scope of cashpoints and online banking to expand their business among what they saw as technologically challenged Indian customers. Kamath drew inspiration from the culture and methodologies of Silicon Valley and turned an insipid industrial lender into a global banking powerhouse, as is evident when you realize that its market capitalization of today is almost 20 times more than in the late 1990s.

Needless to say, ICICI's exceptional story centers on recognizing the limitations and opportunity that India presents by taking into account the necessity to service the needs of millions of low-income consumers in a cost-effective way, while at the same time allying itself closely with the country and complementing the meteoric rise of the Indian economy. The decision to expand ICICI's base globally was also born out of this simple urge to be close to the Indian customer whichever part of the world they are in.

ICICI's presence in western markets has also proven the ideal channel for those seeking to make investments in India or Indians abroad looking to participate in the Indian growth story.

Sitting in his top-floor office at the gleaming ICICI Towers in the Bandra Kurla Complex in Mumbai, Kamath explains:

> "Very simply, our business is to be an anchor for the economic growth of the country. What keeps me going is the challenge of India. It would be very disturbing if the growth story slowed down. A lot of dreams will be upset. We have to fight to keep that dream alive."

Global Vision

Kamath started out by trying to get things right in the domestic consumer credit market. He not only achieved this, but soon became a leader in the competitive housing, auto, and retail credit markets. ICICI also grew to be the largest issuer of credit cards and then made successful forays into insurance, private equity, venture funding, securities, and investment banking by partnering with some of the largest financial services companies in the world, such as the UK's Prudential and Canada's Lombard, to provide life and general insurance services in India. Both the resulting companies, ICICI Prudential and ICICI Lombard, are market leaders in the country.

Not content with serving merely the Indian consumer, domestically or overseas, Kamath spotted the opportunity to advise and finance Indian companies making acquisitions abroad. He began opening up branches, subsidiaries and representative offices across the Americas, Europe, the Middle East, and Southeast Asia to make this global story a real possibility. With CNN broadcasting on a plasma TV in the background, reaffirming his need for breaking news about his clients across the globe, he explains:

"What started out as a need to be near the corporate customer in a global context became our advantage as Indian
companies began showing a large appetite for global assets.
As they became asset acquirers, being known to them gave
us an inside track."

His voracious appetite for expansion took him further as ICICI,
based on its core domestic strength of driving down the costs of
transactions, became one of the first Indian banks to cross over to
a non-Indian consumer market in countries such as Canada, the
UK, and Germany. Non-Indians now form the bulk of its customer
base, primarily those after high savings rate products who are often
referred to as "rate tarts" by the tabloid media. Significantly, ICICI
leads most league tables in the personal finance sections of newspapers and over the past three years has acquired a reputation for
offering the most consistent savings rate in the UK market, beating traditional banks hands down on their own turf. Kamath says:

"Initially it was the NRIs [non-resident Indians] and Indian
businesses that took us abroad, but once we were there, we
found that we could leverage our other competencies. If we
are able to run technology for 10 percent of what it costs
other banks and handle a large volume of customers online,
why shouldn't we operate internet banking in the other
countries we operate in? By back-ending costs to India,
we've found we can save around 75 basis points in operating
costs, and we are passing part of that to the customer in
higher deposit rates so that people are happy to come to us.
The global opportunities are looking much bigger and more
interesting than they did in the beginning."

The bank's other key strength lies in cross-selling products to
Indians abroad. Many of them plan to head back to their home
country at some point in the future and turn to ICICI for financing for property and other investments in India. Kamath adds:

"It is important to understand local nuances. Essentially what we did was take the lessons we learnt in India and applied them globally. But that works in reverse as well and we apply lessons learnt abroad to our business here. All best practices we have are rolled out the world over.

"That is the reason we are global winners. All we have done is sort out the Indian opportunity and serve it in a global context. 90 percent of this opportunity was available to any global player, only 10 percent can be attributed to the Indian back end. We just knew how to use it."

It is Kamath's ability to connect his deep experience of India with the necessity of understanding global money flows that has helped ICICI through the turbulence in the financial markets. Unlike other major international banks such as Citibank and Royal Bank of Scotland, it has had the strength to resist offers of government assistance. This is despite the fact that at the height of rumors about its potential failure, queues formed outside its branches in cities like Chennai, Hyderabad, and Bangalore, resulting in what can only be described as a run on the bank. Prompt actions and timely support from the Reserve Bank of India and the Finance Ministry helped carry the bank through this intense period.

As evidence of the interdependence of the global economy, it was ICICI's UK exposure of $80 million in relation to the collapse of AAA*-rated Lehman Brothers that precipitated the scare-mongering in India. The British Chancellor of the Exchequer even went on live television to state that ICICI was relatively safe and that deposits made through its no-frills internet savings account Hi-Save were safe, when its nearest and more aggressive Icelandic competitors had bitten the dust.

ICICI had one of the highest capital ratios, was fully regulated by the Financial Services Authority, and had a sharp focus on customer service. For example, it made a goodwill payment of £50 per customer as a result of an internet glitch that froze its website. By taking such action, it demonstrated the long-term commitment to international customers that Kamath has long championed and resulted in a new wave of confidence among savers in Britain.

Given the fact that at one stage thousands of customers were queuing outside its branches in India and the news channels were making a bad situation worse by providing 24/7 coverage that could have brought the bank to its knees, Kamath led from the front in recognizing the threat and dismissed fears about its financial instability, stressing they were "baseless and malicious rumors." Knowing he had to put a stop to the speculation, he commenced legal action against various broker networks and others who were fueling the fire.

Having already announced his plans to retire as MD and CEO by Spring 2009, he offered to withdraw his resignation and stay at the helm to see ICICI through a crucial period – again, an important step to reassure customers that the buck stopped with him and that he was willing to shoulder the pain and chart ICICI's course through its troubles.

He succeeded in getting the bank back on a smooth course, evident in its net profits of Rs 41.58 billion for the fiscal year 2008, up from Rs 31.10 billion in the preceding year. The Lehman losses were recouped by a determined leadership team packed with talent.

After the threat was deemed to have subsided, Kamath explained thoughtfully that the upheaval had only strengthened his faith in the resilience of the Indian economy. He predicts:

"While difficulties experienced in global markets and the challenge of domestic inflation driven by global factors and supply-side constraints would continue to test the economy's resilience, we are confident that strong factors of domestic demand and global competitiveness would continue to support high growth rates for the foreseeable future. We will see an environment of single-digit lending rates and double-digit growth about a year from now."

His strategy for the future will take into account a shrinking retail banking sector and focus on mergers and acquisitions to expand further. ICICI's glittering launch in New York, where it acquired branch status in early 2008, marked a watershed for the bank and a personally satisfying achievement for Kamath. Its entry into Germany was followed by the bank's high-profile brand ambassador, Shah Rukh Khan, performing to Bollywood beats for its most affluent clients. The star has proved crucial during the recent turmoil, in a country that takes its Bollywood stars very seriously. Germany has the largest Khan fan base outside of India, but not all international markets have proven as easy.

An ongoing lawsuit in Hong Kong over some of its private banking products and uncertain markets in Russia and Sri Lanka are some of the future hurdles to overcome. Fiscal year 2009 will be critical for ICICI as it plans a strategy shift to depend less and less on agents and deal directly with customers.

Background

Born in 1947 to K Vishwanath and Uma Kamath, K V Kamath spent most of his childhood in Mangalore, Karnataka. His strong entrepreneurial spirit comes from his father, who ran a successful roof tile production and selling business and yet, like most Indians, found enough time for social work. From his mother Kamath learnt the power of introspection and looking for solutions outside the ordinary. One thing both his parents had in common was their unfaltering lesson about the importance of aiming high and achieving a leadership position in whatever field one chooses. Kamath recalls:

"My dad had a small independent business which I helped run for him for a few years while I was studying. It gave me a good picture of how to balance a whole lot of things, people and profits. It was like being thrown into the deep end but that stood me in good stead for years to come."

It was this lesson of never shirking a challenge that stayed with him through his years at St. Aloysius school in Mangalore, mechanical engineering at the Karnataka Regional Engineering College (now the National Institute of Technology, Karnataka), and MBA training at the prestigious Indian Institute of Management, Ahmedabad.

The two years at IIM-A helped develop his skills as a business leader of the future. He became famous for his sheer brilliance on campus. The tale of him submitting his Written Analysis and Communication assignment well before the deadline and yet scoring the highest grade became nothing short of mythical, as even the best of minds struggled with these dreaded work sheets. His proficiency, diligence, and speed during those early years stood him in good stead when he was ready to take on the world of business.

Business

After graduating from IIM-A in 1971, Kamath started his career with ICICI in the project finance division. A year later he married Rajalakshmi, the daughter of a coffee estate owner in Coorg, and set about building a future for his family.

His initial responsibilities at ICICI included business development, credit evaluation, product delivery, project monitoring, syndication, and merchant banking. He eventually took over as executive assistant to the then Chairman, S S Nandkarni, a key inspirational figures in his life until 1985. Kamath subsequently moved to general management positions, set up ICICI's strategic planning division and planned its diversification into the new business areas of investment banking, venture capital, and credit rating.

It was around this time that Kamath initiated the bank's computerization program. Substantial investments in technology right from the late 1980s resulted in systems that are now a competitive advantage for the bank. His consultancy work during this phase opened up new horizons and in 1988 he joined the Asian Development Bank (ADB) in its private-sector department.

For six years he set about gaining experience in Southeast Asian markets, with projects in India, China, Indonesia, the Philippines, Bangladesh, and Vietnam. He was ADB's representative on the boards of several companies and this experience offered additional insight into the workings of global firms.

In 1994, Kamath left ADB to take up the role of adviser to the chairman of Bakrie Group, one of the largest diversified groups in Indonesia. His role was primarily with the financial services operations of the group, which comprised a bank, a finance company, two insurance companies, a securities firm, and a money brokerage.

In 1996, he returned to become Managing Director and Chief Executive Officer at ICICI, taking over from Narayanan Vaghul. He says:

> "My time at ADB gave me exposure to economies in Southeast Asia at a time when they were transforming very rapidly. That experience of looking at those economies and early-day China was a tremendous plus for me. I would have missed out on that perspective had I not gone there. But then it was time to come back to ICICI and I could build on all that I had learnt under Mr. Nandkarni and Mr. Vaghul. They were both sharp minds, thought laterally, delegated a lot, and were true institution builders."

The power of lateral thinking and delegation remain the two cornerstones of his success as a business leader. His hard work and vision were recognized with a Padma Bhushan, one of India's highest civilian honors, in 2008. His role and substantive contribution as the President of the Confederation of Indian Industry, India's premier business association, at a time of economic turmoil have been key factors in his recognition globally.

As CEO, Kamath looked to the likes of Jack Welch, erstwhile CEO of US giant General Electric, and Reliance founder Dhirubhai Ambani for direction. He says:

"The practices that Jack Welch brought into GE may not all have been innovations, but the way he fit them all in makes him an all-time favorite for a lot of CEOs. In terms of entre-preneurial spirit, Dhirubhai is someone I have immense admiration for. He demonstrated for the first time in India that despite all constraints you can grow. He was operating in the days of a closed economy, when most people would accept that there is very little opportunity to grow, but he believed there was a horizon beyond. That strikes me as a very interesting model of leadership,"

Taking Jack Welch's lead on talent differentiation, Kamath put in place groupings for ICICI's HR pool, in which those in the first banding would clearly be groomed for leadership positions – a prime example of his bias for action.

Kamath is believed to have been instrumental in brokering peace between Dhirubhai's heirs, Indian billionaire brothers Mukesh and Anil. His humble acknowledgment of his central role in one of India's most high-profile family disputes was:

"My role is to get people to communicate. Both most cer-tainly talk to me and I talk to them and that process continues."

Turning Point

Kamath set out to establish new horizons for ICICI. He cut his teeth in the big league when the Reserve Bank of India reduced the reserve requirement for the banking sector in the face of crashing interest rates. Between 1996 and 1998 he set about buying large non-banking finance companies, ending in the acquisition of the Bank of Madura.

He went a step further in 2003 by amalgamating the parent institutional lending agency, ICICI, with the ICICI Bank, the largest merger deal at the time. To make the merger possible and meet the central bank's reserve requirements, ICICI had to raise a whopping Rs 230 billion. As a corollary, it had to create a new secondary market for securitized loans amounting to over Rs 80 billion. It also had to liquidate its "sticky" loans by bargaining hard with defaulters and using innovative deals such as land for loan repayment.

The strategy proved successful and ICICI came out on top. Kamath stresses:

"There are several goalposts you set for yourself and reaching those becomes the most satisfying moment for that point of time. The merger between the parent company and the bank we wanted to achieve right from 1996 and when it happened it was a very significant goal post. All the opportunities we planned to bring as a bank have been possible because we were able to achieve the status of a merged entity."

Everything prior to that had been moving toward this ultimate goal, including a listing on the New York Stock Exchange in 2000. Once he had achieved his first big milestone, Kamath was ready to embark on his expansion strategy with a vengeance. His belief in the strength of technology ensured that ICICI was way ahead in terms of hardware and software capabilities. The centrality of technology in ICICI's success is reflected in the fact that Kamath had adopted the role of Chief Information Officer as part of his duties at the bank. He explains:

"I naturally like to observe things and learn from them. It was obvious that technology costs as in the West were not viable for us, but by the mid-1990s as the power of PCs and stand-alone systems started growing, costs fell by half and we had the answer to our technology challenge. We decided this is what we will bet on, stood steadfast in acquiring these systems and it proved the right thing to do.

"Ultimately, I was responsible for technology. It was my neck on the line. We decided we had to run technology in a radically different way so we don't have a technology department or a glorious title like CIO. Technology is embedded in every aspect of the business and the head of the business runs the technology. There is a small group that reported to me and we would discuss any critical plan in technology, be it hardware or software."

This hands-on approach to technology extends into the field of training and flows into his very own work ethic of "bias for action."

Key Strategy

As you may have figured out, Kamath leads by example when it comes to taking action. His key mantra is delegation, which is also responsible for creating a strong talent pool within the organization who take pride in the ICICI way of working. Kamath takes a very personal interest in the hiring process at the higher end of the management spectrum, but steps in only at the very last stage once all his subordinates have given the nod. The idea is to ascertain the person's "soft attributes," such as work ethic and upbringing, to determine whether he or she will fit well within this fast-paced organization. Kamath comments:

"The starting point is to create the proper field where people can show a bias for action. You need to create conditions in the organization that are conducive, for example HR practices, delegation, evaluation, and promotion. How you look at risk taking, where are the checks and balances, and how much leeway do you give people, all determine whether you can create a bias for action.

"That is the reason I take a personal interest in training. In today's world everyone is obsolete in about a year's time. You have to keep refreshing yourself in terms of what you know and don't know. I give myself roughly 10 days to master anything new. Some of it can be literally classroom-style training, some can be through seminars and industry leaders' meets. They all push you into thinking a certain way you may not have before."

A regular at Microsoft chief Bill Gates' annual CEOs' meeting every May, Kamath came up with some of his key working theories through this open-minded approach to business. He is famous for his ability to reinvent himself and his business every two or three years, something he sees as inevitable in a world where anything can be obsolete in a year and the marketplace is changing every other year.

This reinvention led him to clock on to the 90-day rule at a McKinsey seminar. He was convinced that he could apply the same principle of setting up a new system from start to finish within 90 days. He says:

"The discovery that we could apply the speed rule to our projects was a big discovery for our organization. Speed became another important driver in our expansion strategy along with human, financial, and technology capital. It is all a mindset issue rather than a practical one. You have to believe it can be done. Of course, it can't be taken as a dogma and has to be tempered according to the situation, but once the workforce is open to the idea it pushes the entrepreneurial spirit even further.

"I by and large believe in being a macro leader, allowing people at various levels to build the micro picture. I will step in and course correct if the need arises, but I prefer not to. I think that is the best style of management for an organization growing at the pace we are. If you try and micro-manage, there is a danger of ending up with an overload."

To ensure that the micro picture does not get distorted at any level, Kamath took a conscious decision to ensure that his workforce is packed with talented people who are far removed from a bureaucratic mindset. Many see this as the reason ICICI is known for having women in positions of power on the corporate ladder, with leaders like Lalita Gupte, Madhabi Puri Buch, and Shikha Sharma all having had senior executive appointments at the top table. This is not only at the top: Kamath has championed an equally robust but meritocratic intake of women at entry level, in a country where equality for women in the workplace continues to be an uphill struggle.

As further evidence of Kamath's egalitarian nature, his deputy, Ms. Chanda Kochhar, was named as his successor in December 2008, another major first for an Indian bank and unusual for the banking sector internationally. He does not find ICICI's reputation for employing so many women in high posts unusual in any way:

"It is a natural part of putting a meritocracy process in place that throws up so many women leaders. I strongly believe that if you are truly following a process that is very driven, a large number of women will come into leadership roles. None of it is a conscious move. The moment it has to be a conscious effort, it loses its value."

The company's HR strategy reflects this natural drift toward attracting the best. The fast-expanding nature of the group makes this process easier, with young graduates finding ICICI the perfect ground for taking on challenging roles. Kamath says:

"The work needs to be interesting and challenging enough, but also you have to ensure that there is enough delegation. Young people must be given the opportunity to think and do things for themselves or they are going to become mere bureaucrats. They must also be compensated appropriately, but not outrageously. Attrition is a major challenge in India at this point, so we also run on a little extra talent pool so that they can easily be moved around.

"ICICI has a history of allowing its employees a degree of freedom to be entrepreneurs. In the late 1980s we gave it a further push by building new institutions, particularly in the consumer credit market. Each aspect of that required an entrepreneurial spirit, be it credit cards, mortgage, or auto finance. We picked leaders who we believed would be able to perform, thrive on delegation, can take independent decisions, and build a good team.

"The important thing was to move away from any scope of a bureaucratic mindset that works on orders and has to grapple with layers on layers of management. It is not too difficult to move from entrepreneurial to bureaucratic, all it requires is a few processes to destroy the entire ethos of the company."

How else could one explain the success of lieutenants like Sonjoy Chatterjee in establishing a profitable franchise across the western world at such break-neck speed and with such success? Kamath's ability to create leaders has resulted in ICICI's first overseas operation – London – forming the fulcrum for the bank's international ambitions and being used as a launch pad for operations in Germany and Belgium. ICICI UK has more branches than other Indian banks who have been in Britain for over 50 years, has more non-Indian clients, and is praised for offering the UK's most consistent internet "no-frills" savings products.

You could also take the examples of Kalpana Morparia, who after Kamath's grooming took on the CEO's role for JP Morgan in India, or Shikha Sharma, who now heads up Axis Bank, taking to another bank all her learning from successfully building ICICI's retail offering.

At a time when there were fewer than 100 ATMs in India, Kamath decided to carpet-bomb the country with 1,000 ATMs. Experts wondered if this was a slightly crazy move when connectivity was fragile, but Kamath had worked out three levels to cope with that: a dial-up, a leased line, and a satellite link. As for the customers, they were overjoyed that they were saved the hassle of long queues at their local branch for a simple transaction.

The strategy paid off, as ICICI's customer base jumped from 100,000 in 2000 to over 20 million within the next decade.

Indian Perspective

Kamath's ability to forecast consumer needs has time and time again proven correct and has driven innovation in a fairly staid market. Being able to spot trends will determine the success of the next big goal of bringing "banking to the unbanked." The majority of India's population lives in remote rural areas with very little access to capital. Kamath's dream to take banking to this customer base comes from his inclusive nature and deep-seated commitment to the country's progress.

Under his stewardship, ICICI has undoubtedly become a universal juggernaut that caters as much to the poor farmer as to the billionaire businessman. Despite this, he expresses his anguish at not reaching out to as many as he could have, but hopes to leave a legacy that ensures that his dream of reaching the masses is fulfilled. He explains:

"There are 600 million people in India with no banking facilities at all. They live in 600,000 villages spread over 600 districts. We aren't as deep as we would like to be. We have gone purposely down market because we want to provide service to a variety of customers. All our learnings so far we have to take deeper into rural India, where delivery platforms have to be different.

"There is no point in trying to set up shop for deposits because they don't have the money. You have to learn to lend within this small ticket size and make it worthwhile. One product will eventually lead to another. It will require cheaper technology and a partnership model with micro-credit institutions. That is the next big horizon for us."

He takes great pride in how far the "Made in India" brand has come in his lifetime and would like to stress some of the lessons India can teach the globalizing world. The country's unique mind-set of creating things at low cost comes from the constraint of being at a lower level of development. It becomes important to make things available to the population at an affordable cost, but this is also India's biggest advantage, as it instills the ability to think and do things differently. This, according to Kamath, is its competitive advantage:

"The 'Made in India' brand did not have the same connotation a few years ago, but today the focus has shifted to our technological prowess. There has been a rebranding and a lot of that comes from the Indian work ethic which we all grow up with. This hard-working ethos has opened up huge opportunities in an international milieu. We Indians also come with a strong bias for ethics, which is important for any country's growth."

Kamath is keen to invite world players into this country of new opportunities. But he has a few words of caution:

"When you look at India in terms of business, you are looking at an opportunity for the next 20 years and double-digit growth figures. So it has to be a long-term strategy. Also, it is fundamental that you think of India as India. Don't try and work here on Western notions, because ticket sizes are different so cost structures have to be different. As long as you keep these factors in mind, success is guaranteed in India."

Charity

Kamath's strong belief in India's potential has led him to create his own brand of corporate social responsibility (CSR). He is not a big fan of the phrase that has become a buzzword in today's corporate scenario and has his own vision of what needs to be done:

"I feel CSR takes you only thus far and not the whole way through. It is restricted to what you can share with society from your profits, which is a very limited amount. You can hope it becomes a catalyst, touches a few lives, but it does not make transformational change possible.

"For that the answer lies in scalable growth that touches a whole mass of people. For instance, change in rural India that will affect a whole lot of poor. And this change has to be commercial, but in a way that is meaningful to the recipient. This can be done by creating availability and affordability of whatever you are providing.

"Micro-finance lending is an example of this transformational element, where funding is made available to people with no previous access to funds but at a rate they can afford. This will act as a catalyst for change."

His developmental goals include tackling the problem of climate change, but ICICI remains in line with most Indian organizations in not yet taking an official stance on the issue. Kamath, a strong supporter of the India–US nuclear deal as an alternative to meeting India's fuel needs, explains:

"With any such challenge it is important to sift the chaff from the grain. We do believe there is a challenge, but how serious it is has to be worked out. We will develop a strategy as we go along. Waste is definitely a big challenge, depletion of resources is another but as for global warming, we need to understand a little more by separating hype from reality."

China

Unlike many other industry leaders, Kamath has refrained from falling for the hype around China's enormous growth. He wants to assure the world that India does not face competition from this giant neighbor. He says:

"We have an office in China, but in light of the huge opportunities in other places we have to look at China accordingly. India and China are both countries with vast opportunities and we should learn to live with each other. The focus should be on increasing our two-way trade and tourism. Several places in China are closer from Kolkata than other places in India."

While China is at a higher level of development, it is India's position at a lower peg on the developmental scale that is its big advantage, according to Kamath. It brings India a huge cost advantage in terms of keeping human costs significantly lower.

He is confident that India is unstoppable on the path it has set out on, but also warns of the dangers of not containing the divide between rich and poor.

Future Proofing

The most important factor in preventing this growth momentum from slowing down within ICICI is Kamath's focus on hiring and putting talented people at various levels of authority. This goes hand in hand with his dedication to diversification. He says:

> "Getting the right people is a long-term process that we embarked on nearly a decade ago and it is paying off now as they are ready to take the company into the future. We learnt our lessons from being a single-product company long ago and now that we have moved away from that it is time to reap the benefits. We are a provider of a wide range of products, right from the rural to international horizon. This ensures our growth into the next era."

Kamath believes strongly that this platform of growth is open to every player that embraces the challenge of India.

Foreign banks have a common gripe with what they perceive as the closed nature of the Indian financial sector. He disagrees:

> "It is a myth that the Indian financial sector is not open. It is virtually wide open in the field of asset management, securities, and non-bank finance companies. In the banking business there is a limitation on the number of branches, but that exists for any Indian or non-Indian player. It will have to open up gradually."

He never let these constraints stand in the way of hitting the #1 slot in the Indian private banking sector. However, he insists that was never his aim but more an incidental bonus.

Now that he has got ICICI to this pole position, he wants to ensure that it carries on running under its own steam. In true unconventional mode, he turned to a business school professor, Wayne Brockbank from the University of Michigan's Ross School of Business, to collate data on a shortlist of candidates suitable to take over as CEO after him. In 2005, ICICI Bank Chairman N Vaghul, along with Kamath, drew up a list of 12 senior officials from the group who were potential candidates to lead the bank.

Brockbank helped bank officials create a detailed profile of the shortlisted officials.

In December 2008, as a result of Kamath's originality and the process that he kickstarted, Joint Managing Director Chanda Kochhar was named as Kamath's successor. From May 2009, Kamath stepped back and became Non-Executive Chairman to let his female colleague take the lead. As his 13-year action-packed tenure at the helm comes to a close, he explains:

"I will not be continuing with ICICI in an executive role. Beyond that, whether I have a role here or not will be a call that the shareholders and board members will have to take. It would be presumptuous on my part to make a comment on that. But if I am asked to serve, I will certainly consider it positively. As far as leadership is concerned, we have groomed a set of leaders.

"ICICI has responded to all the opportunities and that is where Team ICICI came to the fore. Our team grew in confidence, each member acquiring a unique personality over the years, and today you have a new leader."

Family

Kamath's private life reflects the same matter-of-fact approach. While most of his employees are convinced he is a complete workaholic, he knows exactly when to switch off. Halfway home he stops taking any work calls or even thinking about work. He switches back on halfway to work the next day. In between he can be found pottering around the house, spending time with his wife, son, and daughter, or watching cricket on television. He says:

"Retirement is a state of mind. Back in 1994, I felt I had built my little nest egg and achieved some goals so I decided

I would stop working. But that didn't happen as I decided to come back to ICICI. There are just so many things I want to do that there is no time to take a break."

With a global regulatory framework for financial services being mooted by senior members of the G20, Kamath's unique experience at the Asian Development Bank and ICICI stands him in good stead to contribute and lead the process. He would be able to provide a perspective that encompasses an understanding of the economies of the developed world with experience of a booming India and other Southeast Asian tiger economies that are regularly talked of as the future of the world.

If ever a banker with entrepreneurial credentials and a bias for action is required, I'm sure the world knows where to find him.

Kiran Mazumdar-Shaw

- Chairman of Asia's largest biotechnology company, the world's 7th largest biotech employer, with global sales of $712 billion and a presence in 75 countries.
- Formed her company in a garage after her preferred career as a master brewer hit a glass ceiling due to her gender.
- Listed her company in 2004 to become India's wealthiest female entrepreneur.
- Vociferous critic of politicians, especially from Bangalore, whose inaction, she claims, has resulted in the silicon valley of India's reputation being tarnished due to its short-sighted infrastructural development and crumbling public utilities.

Healing the World

Imagine for a moment a woman who, despite an international education and professional achievements, was unable to convince her employers to entrust her with running the show. Imagine the moment she decided that enough was enough and chose to quit. Imagine the impact of such a vote of no confidence on her character and her sense of personal failure when she realized that she couldn't break through the glass ceiling. All because she was a woman at a time when sociocultural norms in India were that women stayed at home and served the needs of their family.

Nevertheless, realizing that her education need not be wasted, Kiran Mazumdar-Shaw set about applying her knowledge of brewing and fermentation not to the production of alcoholic beverages, but to the production of medicines. By doing so, she gave birth to an entirely new industry of which she is the undisputed leader, earning the title of the "Queen of Biotech" from *The Economist* and *Fortune*.

It would be fair to suggest that she set up Biocon India at a time when few in India knew what biotech really meant. And her lack of experience and gender both conspired against her. As a 25-year-old entrepreneur, she was not only stepping into a largely male-dominated world, but also into a field that was a risky proposition. From the very basic problems of getting the finance she required to convincing men to work under her management, it all began as an uphill struggle.

Not one to shy away from adversity, with an initial capital of just $250 and a small garage space in the South Indian city of Bangalore as her only assets, Mazumdar-Shaw set about creating the Indian arm of a successful Irish business in 1978 and founded India's biotech industry. Living through ups and downs parallel with the country's journey of development, she faced all her challenges and as a result of her strongest trait – her persistence –

Biocon India grew into a multimillion-dollar company and successfully listed on the Indian stock market in 2004 for $1.1 billion.

Having dominated the domestic market, Mazumdar-Shaw has her eyes set on conquering the four corners of the world by acquiring complementary businesses. She understands the company's fundamental differentiator better than anyone else: quite simply, Biocon can develop therapeutics for diseases such as cancer and diabetes at a far lower and more affordable cost than its bigger rivals. This is the kind of factor that is crucial to a company's survival in an economic downturn. Mazumdar-Shaw explains:

"The power of biotechnology is that it is cheap and effective. It mimics the body's way of dealing with disease. When we got into the insulin business, it instantly slashed the cost of insulin for diabetics in India and around the world. We are now working on creating an oral insulin that will completely revolutionize the treatment of diabetes. These are the things that give me a high, finding innovative ways of doing things."

Global Vision

Given the importance of the US market, India celebrated when Biocon became the first Indian company to get the nod of the US Food and Drugs Administration for its fermentation-derived molecules for pharmaceutical use. A very important door had opened for an industry that held so much promise for Indian enterprise.

In 2007, Mazumdar-Shaw decided it was time to step away from enzymes and focus entirely on research and development-based biopharmaceuticals, including active pharmaceutical ingredients (APIs), biologicals, and proprietary molecules. The sale of its enzymes business to Denmark's Novozymes for an estimated $115 million marked the take-off point for Biocon's global ambitions.

The company's Chairman and Marketing Director has since been on a buying spree around the world. After gaining a foothold in the European market with the acquisition of German drug marketing firm AxiCorp in 2008, Biocon set its sights on the US pharma distribution market. It also set up a joint venture company in Dubai, along with Abu Dhabi-based drug maker Neopharma, to develop and market biopharmaceutical products for treating diseases such as cancer, diabetes, obesity, and heart ailments in the Middle East market. Mazumdar-Shaw, whose appetite for expansion has proved insatiable, says:

"It has been a slow, deliberate process of moving away from enzymes to biopharmaceuticals because that is where the global future of the company lies. We have leveraged a lot of our existing technology platforms to move into this field. India is very good at manufacturing, so all we need are worldwide networks to distribute our products. Since marketing of biopharmaceuticals, especially insulin products, needs special expertise and regional experience, acquiring such infrastructure would be an ideal option.

"In 10 years, I see Biocon's products in all major global markets. Already 60 percent of our products are sold globally, but they are mostly in raw material form. It is time we create the tablets and vials that clearly identify us in these markets. We want to target areas where there are no cures or where existing options have nasty side effects."

Undeterred by the fact that the global economic meltdown makes this a difficult climate in which to realize her expansion ambitions, she adds:

"The challenge for the future is cost reduction in drug development. Competing in the new world order has a new meaning. It is about delivering the highest-quality generics and biosimilars at the lowest cost. In the research services sector, it is about being able to deliver increasingly higher-value services cost effectively."

She is certain about not resorting to cuts in R&D. Innovation, she predicts, will prove the key to surviving the credit crunch. That is probably why Biocon was able to register a 46 percent hike in profits for 2008–09. Mazumdar-Shaw explains:

"Affordable R&D will be key to realizing commercial success. It is here where Indian companies can illuminate a silver lining amidst the gloom. Whilst innovators are experiencing increased difficulty in reimbursements for new drugs, co-development models with companies in India and China are enabling such companies to reduce development costs. Cost of goods is certainly being recognized as key to competing in the global arena, both in terms of biosimilars as well as novel products. There is a gradual but perceptible shift in bio-manufacturing to lower-cost economies."

Background

Born in 1953, Kiran had what she calls a "charmed childhood" in Bangalore. Her father was the Chief Master Brewer and Managing Director of United Breweries, one of India's most famous alcohol giants, now headed by flamboyant millionaire and close family friend Vijay Mallya.

The upper middle-class family enjoyed some wonderful holidays during her school days at Bishop Cotton Girls School and Mount Carmel School in Bangalore. Kiran went on to get a degree in Zoology from Bangalore University.

Her father could see that his two younger sons were not inclined toward the biological sciences like his daughter. One went on to become a Professor of Mathematics in Canada and the other a software entrepreneur in Los Angeles. Her father encouraged

Kiran to follow in his footsteps and pursue a career as a Master Brewer, which she accepted with relish and succeeded at, qualifying as a Master Brewer at Ballarat Institute of Advanced Education, now University of Ballarat, Australia. She recalls:

> "My father was always someone who had implicit belief in what his daughter could do. He felt that I was someone very special. He realized that neither of his sons were interested in life sciences and that made our relationship even closer, because we shared common interests and were headed towards a common profession."

Soon after returning from Australia, Kiran was faced with the realities of the male chauvinistic world of brewing in India. She had interned at Carlton & United Breweries in Melbourne as a Trainee Brewer in 1974, but it became clear to her that there was no way to break through the glass ceiling in India.

However, that was to ultimately work in her favor when her expertise in fermentation science and technology proved useful in a field completely unrelated to brewing. She explains:

> "My father was definitely disappointed that I could not pursue a career in brewing. He was aware it was not due to any fault of mine and felt people were silly to let an opportunity pass when there was a dearth of Master Brewers in India. But I had realized my gender was working against me. Most brewers and brewery owners were very reluctant to give the management control of their breweries to a woman. The only way out was to start something of my own.
>
> "I decided to start Biocon in India literally as a rebound, as I didn't get anywhere with brewing. A lot of biotechnology depends on fermentation and I decided to use my expertise in a different field. My father saw me grow the company from scratch and was very proud of what I had achieved."

Her father passed away in 1993, when Biocon was on an upward swing.

Business

The company's journey began through an accidental encounter with Leslie Auchincloss, founder of an Irish biotech company, Biocon Biochemicals. A brewer himself, Auchincloss convinced the young Kiran that she had what it takes to start a biotech business in India. With no financial backing and just Rs 10,000 ($250) as an investment, she set up Biocon India in 1978 as a joint venture.

Using a small garage in Bangalore as the company headquarters – quite a contrast to its glitzy 80-acre campus on Hosur Road in Bangalore today – and with two employees, Mazumdar-Shaw set about building a business that was about manufacturing and exporting enzymes. Her initial remit was to extract papain, an enzyme found in papaya used to make meat more tender, and isinglass, from tropical catfish, which clarifies beer.

Realizing that she was not prepared to do this for the rest of her life, her innovative streak resulted in her developing novel enzymes for industrial uses, food additives, and process aids, which resulted in 15 patents and the potential for mass production for the US and Europe as well as the domestic market.

In order to grow, Mazumdar-Shaw searched for financial backers, only to be disappointed by banks who didn't share her enthusiasm or understand her business. By chance, in conversation with the Chairman of the Industrial Credit and Investment Corporation of India (ICICI), Narayanan Vaghul, she presented her best case and impressed him sufficiently to gain his personal and monetary support. She explains:

"Mr Vaghul is one of the people I admire a lot. He believed in me when I needed money and nobody would touch me. He said he'll back me because he had faith in me and was trying to set up a venture capital fund at ICICI, which proved an ideal starting point for me."

With wind beneath her wings, she proved him right and went from strength to strength. In 1996, she decided to chart a course for Biocon that led to developing strategic biopharmaceuticals; and in 1998, she achieved a major milestone by becoming independent from Biocon's foreign shareholders.

Turning Point

"When I was asked to set up the company, I took it on purely on an experimental basis. I thought, let me see what this enzyme business is all about. My eureka moment came when I realized that it was not all about plant enzymes but a large number of enzymes are produced by microbial fermentation. And I thought, hey I know about fermentation, I have studied it, so why don't I try and apply the same technology to produce enzymes?"

She quickly realized that to achieve her dreams, she needed to focus on the execution of the idea, a set of skills she knew she possessed:

"It was clear what I was planning to do will require a lot of research. That is something not many people were doing in India. So I thought, let me get started on it. I wanted to set up a research base to make novel enzymes and market them the world over. That proved a big challenge and also a strength, as no one in India was doing that. That is what my company is based on now, research and the commercialization of it, and it is all based on fermentation. What an ideal combination!"

It is this unique vision that has transformed Biocon from a low-level industrial enzymes company to a globally integrated biopharmaceutical firm with strategic research initiatives.

In 1994, Mazumdar-Shaw achieved another Indian first by setting up Syngene, a contract research company. Today this entity earns a chunk of Biocon's revenues by partnering on research projects with the world's biggest drug companies, such as Bristol-Myers Squibb and AstraZeneca. Following her success, other Indian companies began to cash in on the new "research process outsourcing" trend.

In 2000, Biocon launched another entity called Clinigene to focus on clinical trials, such as those concerning both generic and novel medicines like an oral insulin to replace the existing injectible and inhalant forms, which will prove a boon for diabetics. Mazumdar-Shaw says:

"Our company's story is of ordinary people who believed they could do great things. Biotech is all about revolutionizing drugs and vaccine production to bring down costs. Businesses such as enzymes and clinical research outsourcing help us generate capital to invest in newer businesses such as new drug discovery."

Key Strategy

Biocon started out as a manufacturer and exporter of enzymes and gradually shifted focus to become a life science-driven generics company exploiting fermentation technology. It is now poised on its newest phase, a transition from a generic drugs firm to a discovery-led life science company. Behind the entire transition process is a very simple guiding philosophy, once expressed by Mazumdar-Shaw's 6-year-old nephew in a school essay: "If I found a pot of gold, I would give it to my aunt so that her company could make new medicines for bad diseases." She was so touched by this sentiment that it has remained her business ideal.

Her bread-and-butter business has been the production of generic drugs, including statins or cholesterol-lowering drugs. Despite stiff competition from Chinese companies, the statins business has continued to grow.

Nevertheless, not one to remain focused on a single strategy, Mazumdar-Shaw began devoting most of her time and energy to being a drug innovator. Her target areas have been monoclonal antibodies (MABs) or cancer vaccines and other drugs related to arthritis. The MABs that Biocon is working on are considered second-generation chimeric or "humanized" MABs, compared to the older murine or rodent-based variants of some of Biocon's competitors.

The project of pride, however, remains the oral insulin, which is expected to hit the market by 2010. The company's R&D chief presented the results of the Phase II clinical study at the European Association for the Study of Diabetics meeting in Rome in 2008.

Indian Perspective

Mazumdar-Shaw's guiding force is her strong urge to put the "Made in India" brand on the global map. Her future expansion plans are inextricably linked to this India factor, about which she says:

> "It has always been my dream to make a global impact with a 'Made in India' label. I think a lot of my generation comes from that frame of reference. We have always had to apologize for India and now is the time we don't want to apologize for our country. We want to be proud of it."

But this urge to make her country proud is not a blind passion. She believes that her cautious steps toward international success are what give her an edge over her competitors. As she describes it:

"Indians by nature are extremely cautious to globalization, we tend not to go about it in an aggressive way. That's just the way we are brought up. Because we were colonized, there is a tendency to be a little subservient. At the same time, Western companies tend to be a bit patronizing. The key is to adapt.

"Indian companies wanting to enter western markets with a rigid Indian viewpoint are unlikely to succeed and the same goes for western companies expanding in India. There has to be a sort of balance. Indians are a little less clinical and focus on the soft aspects and human elements of a business more. This can work heavily in our favor. When I acquire a company, it is first to do with the people. The people chemistry has to be right. The mantra for me is to breed a culture of owning a problem rather than a task."

It is with exactly this clarity that the woman referred to as "India's mother of invention" by the *New York Times* runs Biocon. Determined not to follow the common hierarchical structure of most Indian companies, Mazumdar-Shaw is popular for her unique management style. She fosters a very informal atmosphere where employees are encouraged to speak their mind without fear of being sacked for displeasing the boss. She is often seen chatting to a worker on the floor and believes in keeping her finger on the pulse of every aspect of her business. She comments:

"When I started Biocon, I didn't come with any baggage or preconceived notions of how to manage a company. But there was one thing I was very sure of, that I didn't want a feudal structure like in many Indian companies at the time. What helped me create a unique management style was when I spent six months in Ireland with my partners. There was a lot of informality in the workplace, everyone addressed each other by their first names, a completely alien concept in India. But despite this informality there was a sense of ownership and commitment to the work. I knew I wanted to create a part of this culture back in India. I wanted work to be a fun place where people can express themselves.

"Another important aspect was a lack of hierarchy. It was a very flat, networked organization. I thought, let me give this a shot in India. I knew it would be tough, but from day one I encouraged a very flat, interactive organization. That has remained my style. As the company grows it tends to get structured, but I try very hard to break that down. I am conscious of the fact that I have to set the trend. I go and talk to the junior-most guy on the floor and encourage juniors to come and talk to me. Leadership is about setting the standards and walking the talk.

"I knew I never wanted an organization where no one can question me. My door is always open for people to walk in and share their views with me. So much so that in the early days people often thought I would sack the person seen arguing with me. Now it is clear to everyone that it is just another day at work where people can freely express their opinions. If people tend to hold back, then it either reflects insecurity or a flawed relationship."

On women in the workplace, she explains:

"Knowledge does not have a gender divide – women scientists, women engineers, women writers have enormous opportunities to excel and succeed. At Biocon we do our best to ensure gender sensitivity issues are addressed. Women are encouraged not to come at odd hours in the night and if women have to travel to interior areas of the country, a male escort is provided. Biocon has a fully equipped crèche that enables employees to have their children cared for while they pursue their careers at the workplace. These considerations take care of employee apprehensions. However, I am not the kind of person who will appoint women for the sake of their gender, but for the role they play."

It is this clear-minded approach to her work that has helped Mazumdar-Shaw stand out in a very male-dominated world, which is normally characterized by layers of hierarchy and formality.

Today, she is a larger-than-life presence in her home town of Bangalore, where she is often seen zipping around in a silver Mercedes dressed in her trademark scarves and pearls. Her distinctive booming voice and individual style set her apart as a born leader who refuses even to consider that it's a man's world. Seen as a trailblazer for other aspiring female entrepreneurs, she says:

"The key is success. As you succeed, gender barriers break down. I had a very uphill struggle in terms of credibility issues. Things have changed enormously since, there are a lot more women in business. But families still don't believe girls can pursue a stand-alone career of their own. There are a lot of double standards towards working women, but ultimately it is the women who have to put their foot down and drive that change.

"I believe in being very up-front and honest and extremely fair in dealing with people. You get me as I am; my frankness often rebounds but in most cases it is a big positive. When it comes to work I believe in sharing my vision with the team that I have built around me. I don't believe in holding things back or keeping my cards close to my chest. This openness, I feel, makes people trust me, which is a very important leadership quality when you are trying to grow a company.

"My decisiveness to the point of being impulsive makes me a bit impatient, but it also means my enthusiasm rubs off on people around me."

Charity

This enthusiasm and passion spill over into other areas of life. In 2005, Mazumdar-Shaw set up the Biocon Foundation to identify and implement projects that will influence India's social and economic situation. Its main focus areas are providing quality healthcare and health education for the betterment of Indian society.

Arogya Raksha Yojana (Disease Protection Project) was the first step taken by her charity in this direction. Through this initiative, the foundation provides high-quality drugs at affordable prices to the masses at all BioCare Pharmacies and participating clinics. Working alongside Dr. Devi Shetty, the founder of a unique rural health scheme, this first-of-its-kind initiative has been growing exponentially. Mazumdar-Shaw explains:

"This is a very interesting model we are trying to create of micro health insurance. Health insurance is normally aimed at affluent urban people. Ignoring rural people who form such a big part of the Indian population will cause huge problems in the long run. The objective of Arogya Raksha Yojana is to provide quality healthcare at a reasonable cost to those very masses and root out indebtedness to money-lenders."

Besides healthcare, education is the other cause closest to her heart. In 2006, the Biocon Foundation unveiled a unique mathematics self-help book for primary schools, in collaboration with Macmillan India Limited. The book aims to make mathematics fun for children. She says:

"Biocon Foundation has a strong commitment to promoting education, especially among underprivileged children. We believe an excitement for math, if encouraged at an early age, will go a long way in helping students cope with challenges on the subject in later years."

Mazumdar-Shaw has also been India's ambassador for biotechnology, a role she decided to pursue aggressively at a time when India was not known for biotech. She is the Chairperson of Karnataka's Vision Group on Biotechnology, a Member of the Advisory Council of the Indian Government's Department of Biotechnology, and Vice-President of the Association of Women Entrepreneurs of Karnataka (AWAKE). At the helm of various conferences and delegations, her aim has been to highlight the possibilities that biotech offers to a country like India:

> "I have made a lot of time to address certain key issues. India wasn't really known for biotechnology, so I felt that if I can in some way build a brand for India, it would be very fulfilling."

Another subject about which she feels extremely passionately is the state of the city that has been her home for years. She is behind a number of initiatives to improve what she describes as a "crumbling" city, but has found it quite a frustrating struggle:

> "It really concerns me that a city like Bangalore is breaking down because the government is not doing enough. People in India tend to be really apathetic. I decided to get together with some like-minded people to shake things out of that apathy. There is a huge disconnect between the public and private sector. The latter has zoomed ahead in a world of its own and things in the public sector have not quite kept pace. I sometimes really wish I could be Chief Minister of Bangalore for a year so that I could completely transform the city."

This very active role in public life has often led to her friends expecting her to fight an election, but Mazumdar-Shaw is adamant that she will get more done out of office. Close friend Vijay Mallya's foray into politics served as a lesson for her to stay well away:

"His experiences opened my eyes to a lot of things. He was so excited when he formed a political party [Janata Party] and would call me about the huge groups he had attracted at his election rallies. But he didn't ultimately win even one seat in Parliament. People are not quite ready for us. We come with a very naïve mindset of doing good.

"Politics is a very different business. I have spent a lot of time in rural India, building clinics, community toilets, joining hands with the government to make sure the numerous schemes that are announced are actually implemented. I may be this wonderful person who has transformed their village, but I know very well if I stand for elections, I will not win. The village *panchayat* [local rural government] is so strong that it will never let someone like me in. People tend not to vote for people not seen as politicians."

These concerns for her city and country also encompass more global factors such as climate change, an issue that she is confident needs addressing:

"A lot of us get trapped into making statements on climate change, but very frankly none of us really understands what ought to be done. It is obvious there are problems when the water table is consistently going down and the weather patterns are changing so dramatically. The answer has to be in conservation, such as rainwater harvesting. But talking about carbon credits as a solution is really facetious. I can't help laughing when those whizzing around in their private jets talk about carbon offsetting. It is very hypocritical."

China

This no-nonsense approach to problems has led Mazumdar-Shaw into difficult markets such as China. Biocon's generic drugs business came under severe attack from cheaper Chinese drugs, but she rode that tide with confidence in her firm's superior fermentation skills, while its neighbors were still relying on easy-to-copy synthetic molecules. She says:

"China is a formidable competitor. Chinese vendors definitely made an impact on statin prices in the global market, first by reducing prices marginally by 10 percent and eventually by as much as 40–50 percent. We had to reduce our prices to compete with them. But despite reduced prices, Biocon remained a dominant player across the statin segments and managed not to lose a single customer."

Biocon has maintained its upper hand with a clear-cut expansion strategy in the region. Mazumdar-Shaw adds:

"China is a force to be reckoned with, but it also faces some huge challenges in future. Its population demography will not be great in 20 years. India, if it plays its cards right, can easily score over China. We have the obvious language advantage; no matter how hard they try to learn English, they will never be as comfortable with it as Indians.

"But the biggest positive going for China is a determined government that has put all resources into its development with a single-minded focus. India is growing in all directions, that focus has been lacking. The problem with us is that we get carried away with small successes. This is really the start of our success story.

"The biggest danger we face is this hype around India Inc. There is still one big factor to address and that is infrastructure. All our growth will come crashing down if we don't address the need of roads, airports, ports, and basic amenities to call ourselves a modern country. We can't keep saying we are a great country when there are still villages without a basic sewage system."

Future Proofing

Her business strategy for the future is governed by this very approach. She sees herself as the custodian of Biocon and plans to hand it over to whoever is best capable of running it in the future.

She has a clear focus on where the biopharma industry is headed and plans to steer her company to the right destination, without any plans to slow down or retire. She comments:

"Succession won't be a problem as I have a group of people working with me. I don't worry that this company will collapse after me, it won't. My job is to set the right course. If India Inc. is to attain global leadership in pharmaceuticals, we must recognize and enable the important paradigm shift between manufacturing generics and inventing and commercializing novel drugs.

"Today, the Indian pharma sector is ranked fourth in terms of volume and 13th in terms of value globally. It is imperative that we leverage our intellectual capital to climb up the value chain and it is important that we do it our way as opposed to replicating the model used by the West, which completely forgets the affordability factor.

"Our talent pool combined with our flourishing capital markets that can fund innovation enable us to address the cost and productivity challenges being faced by the developed world. This is our challenge and opportunity to create the start of a 'golden era' for the pharma sector in India. We must not fail our country and its citizens, who all deserve access to affordable medicine."

Family

For a woman on such a mission, it is inevitable that work dominates Mazumdar-Shaw's life. She does find time out for her husband, John Shaw, whom she describes as her anchor. Her ideal way to unwind is to relax with him over a glass of wine with Pavarotti playing in the background.

She underscores the role of family by explaining:

"It is important to have family support and cooperation to succeed in one's career. For women especially, balancing home and work life may become difficult without adequate support from the family. Whilst it is true that I was single when I built Biocon, the real growth came when I got married. My husband has played a vital role in our success today."

She met the Indophile from Scotland when he was Managing Director of Madura Coats in Bangalore. A strong six-year friendship eventually resulted in a life partnership. Their work and family life are perfectly intermingled, as he handles finance and international business at Biocon with his wife. She recalls:

"John and I were good friends in the platonic sense. When he left India in 1997, I realized there was a huge void and vacuum in my life. We have common interests in art and cuisine. I visited him in Holland when I was on a business trip. We then stayed away from each other for two months. And the next time I went to Holland, he proposed to me."

Their mutual love of art has turned their office and Spanish-style villa in Bangalore into mini art galleries.

She also has a very close group of friends and is popular in Bangalore circles for throwing some of the most fun parties. As she says:

"I always make time for my friends over the weekend. I call them as often as I can. Friendship is a very special aspect of one's life and you should never let it slip away."

But work is clearly what gives her a sense of purpose and a code to live by. So much so, that she and her husband took the unconventional decision not to have children. She explains:

"When one is involved with work, it would not be fair to have a child as there will be time constraints. I believe in wealth creation in the form of building intellectual property through which the Indian drug industry can attain sustainable growth. That is the reason I no longer feel embarrassed by the 'wealthiest woman' tag. I always insist that I am not the richest but the wealthiest, because a large part of this wealth is not money but the intellectual wealth I have created, having started off with nothing. Life's not about diamonds and gold but this value creation for the future."

I'm amazed that despite the difficulties she's faced – first with gender equality and secondly when giving birth to an entire new industry in India – she retains a very generous and pragmatic attitude toward work and life in general, making her a truly likable person.

She may be the only woman in this book, but one thing's for sure, her inspiration as a path burner will ensure that we see the success of other Indian female entrepreneurs taking their game to the world over the coming years.

Not many people have built a business from its inception in a garage in an unknown industry sector to a billion-dollar listed company. When Mazumdar-Shaw eventually decides to call it a day, she should take pride in having created a legacy that India itself is proud of.

Subramaniam Ramadorai

- One of Ratan Tata's longest-serving and best-performing lieutenants, in charge of the IT services consultancy company Tata Consultancy Services (TCS).
- TCS is India's largest software company, with worldwide sales worth $5.7 billion per year and consultants in 170 offices across 50 countries.
- Took charge as CEO in 1996 and has transformed the company from one employing 5,000 staff to its strength of 130,000 today from 160 nationalities. Retired in October 2009 to pursue charitable interests and to indulge his love for music.
- In 2009 appointed Vice-Chairman of TCS, and awarded a CBE by Queen Elizabeth II for his contribution to the Indo-British economic relationship.
- Almost two thirds of the Tata Group's profits go to worthwhile charitable causes.

Putting Indian IT on the World Map

From the moment an ordinary Indian wakes up in the morning to when they fall asleep, they are likely to have used at least one product or service provided by the legendary Tata group. It is such penetration that has led 3.2 million Indian investors to back the company, which accounts for around 4.3 percent of the total value of the Bombay Stock Exchange. In India, it's safe to say that everyone knows who the Tatas are.

However, it's only recently that the Tata name has begun registering in the psyche of those living in far-flung countries like the US and the UK. This is despite the fact that the Tatas started their global journey over a century ago: they set up their London office in 1907, in an era when Indian independence seemed a far-away dream.

Fast forward to today and you see an increasing commitment to put down deeper roots, and by doing so demonstrate the group's intent to become a dominant player in its markets globally. Just as we saw the likes of Daewoo and Samsung becoming international players, there's no doubt that we're witnessing the birth of another globally acceptable super-brand, with a stable of 98 companies.

In no small measure, the Tatas' achievements are down to a band of long-serving professional executives who have worked their hearts out to make the company even greater. While recently it has been Jaguar Land Rover, a subsidiary of Tata Motors, that has been creating news, the company that stands out as being the most international is Tata Consultancy Services (TCS), headed until very recently by Subramaniam Ramadorai. To my mind he should take the credit for the rise of this incredibly successful enterprise.

A one-time junior engineer who has become one of the world's leading information technology brains, Ramadorai stepped into the world of computers when many of us would not have even begun to fathom the scope or importance of information technology. Analytical solutions came easily to his science and math-focused brain. He had the unique vision to see beyond the obvious and is today synonymous with India's IT prowess. As Chief Executive Officer, Ramadorai built TCS into a global giant to be reckoned with. Without a doubt, it is on its way to being mentioned in the same breath as other IT giants like IBM, Hewlett-Packard, and Accenture.

During the past 30 years, Ramadorai has played an integral role in the international development of TCS. His efforts have helped make it one of the world's largest global software and services companies, with more than 130,000 associates working in 50 countries and operating out of over 170 offices worldwide. It netted $1 billion in profits in the financial year ending 2007 and expanded its revenues to a whopping $5.7 billion by 2008. As India's largest IT services provider, it has a palpable impact on everyday life, from supermarket checkout counters to complex banking solutions. Ramadorai says:

> "The opportunity to shape the future is the hallmark of the Tata Group, be it in steel, textile, hotels, energy, or IT. In the days I joined as a trainee, IT was unheard of and had hardly any role to play in the Indian context. But having seen its application and scope in the US, I was confident that some day it could be used to build key solutions around it in India as well."

Global Vision

After taking on the role of CEO in 1996, Ramadorai focused his efforts on building relationships with large corporations and academic institutions, planning and directing technology development and acquisitions, and overseeing the company's research and development activities.

He played a pioneering role in establishing offshore development centers to provide high-end solutions to major corporations, including General Electric, Morgan Stanley, American Express, Merrill Lynch, Capital Bank, Target Corporation, Citibank, Ericsson, and Nortel. Under his leadership TCS also set up technology excellence centers in India that have acquired knowledge, expertise, and equipment in specialized technology areas.

He spearheaded TCS's quality initiatives, taking 16 of its development centers to the coveted Capability Maturity Model (CMM) Level 5, the highest and most prestigious performance assessment issued by the Software Engineering Institute. Over 22,000 TCS employees have been covered by this assessment. TCS also attained the distinction of being the world's first company to have all centers assessed as operating at Level 5 of PCMM (People-CMM). Ramadorai says:

"I very strongly believe we are global winners. Our global visibility is helping us a lot. The Tata Group adds a lot to our credibility, especially after our global acquisition deals with Corus, Jaguar, and Land Rover. We are recognized for our engineering and innovation. We are very visible as a brand."

And his confidence is well placed. As an example of its international success, since 2004 Ferrari and TCS have been working together to make sure that the Formula 1 race cars deliver their best performance on the race track week after week. As competition becomes hotter between the teams, computers and technology are increasingly seen as central factors in gaining pole position. Ferrari has turned to TCS to help with software development, spanning soft simulation of the actual race track and telemetry that allows it to record the car's behavior in all conditions. With such a fast-paced sport, it comes as no surprise that TCS needs to update or write new software code for Ferrari every one or two weeks in order to keep it in the game.

Ramadorai comments:

"We have repeatedly demonstrated engineering and process rigor and have built an institutionalized framework for attention to detail. Our engineering and unigraphic capabilities built over 20 years appealed to Ferrari. We have had a very satisfying relationship where we are treated as equal partners and an extension of their team. There can be no room for changes when a race is on and our quality engineering capability is what Ferrari needs."

TCS's engineering practice, of which the Ferrari account is the most prestigious, contributes around 6 percent of the company's revenues. The engineering vertical also includes aerospace, heavy engineering, and automotive. In aerospace, another high-tech sector, Boeing is one of the key customers. TCS has a center of excellence for engineering in Pune and another for aerospace at Bangalore.

Background

Commenting on his formative years, Ramadorai starts by philosophizing:

"You know, as a child I loved flying kites. I loved the challenge of a good start, the moment of release when it rode the wind to rise higher and higher. I loved the brightly colored paper machines dancing and swaying in the breeze, it really gave me a thrill. Perhaps there was a deeper meaning, quite unknown to me at that time."

Born in Nagpur, Maharashtra, in 1944 into a South Indian middle-class family, he was fed a diet of scientific and mathematical analysis. He honed his skills as a young of student in New

Delhi and went on to acquire a bachelor's degree in physics from Delhi University; a bachelor of engineering degree in electronics and telecommunications from the Indian Institute of Science in Bangalore; and a master's degree in computer science from the University of California. He says:

"Logic, analytical capabilities and maths was something we grew up with. I found physics, as a subject, very analytical. My own personal growth at home and at the various educational institutions was always tuned to that. As a family, science and maths always formed the hallmark for everything we did. Even something like music, which I grew up with at home, as an area I found highly mathematical. My move into computer science was a natural process.

"Much to my dislike then, there were more serious and scholarly pursuits to follow. A traditional upbringing placed great importance on education. This saw me ultimately reach the US in 1969. A journey so long... from Mumbai to Kolkata, Bangkok, Manila, Saigon, Tokyo, Honolulu, and finally Los Angeles, over 40 hours of travel in all. At the end of it all I wanted to do in the so-called land of dreams was to get a glass of water and some sleep.

"America then was a cultural shock for a country bumpkin like me, every day was a learning experience. But learn I did. It certainly broadened my horizons and made me more self-reliant."

Having completed his education, Ramadorai was settling in to a cushy job in the US when he was offered the chance to take over as a junior engineer at the newly formed TCS in 1972. A 26-year-old with bright plans for the future, he saw it as an opportunity not to be missed. He recalls:

"Way back in 1968, when I left for the US for higher studies, we always used to look at two potential job opportunities in

India: one was the government administrative services and the second was joining the Tata Group. Tata has always been billed as a phenomenal employment opportunity. So based on the TCS offer, I decided it was time to return to India. I was doing well; there was no need for me to return to India. I had a job in the US and enough economic and immigration reasons to stay there, but personally I took the step to come back because I felt this job would put me in a position to learn and apply technology for the future."

He adds in a lighter tone that his parents also provided extra motivation to return to India:

"My parents then kind of clinched the deal, when they told me they had found a pretty girl for me. So family pressures and the lure of marriage brought me back. I am so glad I went back, for there I found my life partner. Or should I say life partners – professional and personal. Of course, Mala never fails to remind me of 'my marriage to TCS' as she calls it."

Business

From day one, Ramadorai felt himself fitting in comfortably into the ethos of TCS. He enjoyed the sense of initiative it gave him. There was a lot of optimism about possible strategies for the future. He explains:

"My first day at work was rather uneventful. Most visionary companies don't have a very formal process of telling you what you are supposed to do. When you are coming back from the US, everything is a very highly process-oriented culture with someone briefing you at every step of the way and an HR person showing you the way.

"It was a complete change that no one meets you and leaves you wondering what to do. I learnt very quickly that if you keep waiting, you will be permanently waiting. I had to jump into various aspects of the business fairly quickly under my own steam. I met my boss only two weeks after joining. That was my first very important lesson: don't expect anyone to seek you out and tell you what to do. Take the initiative."

On finally meeting his boss, F C Kohli, he remarks:

"Briefly after having joined Tata's I met Kohli. He was a tough taskmaster, but as I learnt later he had a soft heart. He was a man of few words, his instructions were minimal, and it taught me a great lesson to be a good listener and to anticipate what was required. He threw challenge after challenge, stretching us towards continuous improvement, at the same time giving a wide scope for experimentation. I was hungry to learn so although a part of me wanted to just walk away, I stuck on and faced them. Always an excellent foot soldier, I recollect days when we did a 4.30 a.m. to 11.30 p.m. beat in the US meeting customers. Times like these helped us establish a comfortable relationship between us."

On the importance of the US and his stints there, he says:

"I found myself back in the US in 1979 to set up TCS's operation there. One person who was not amused at all was Naval Mody, head of what was then Tata Incorporated. He was very skeptical about what I was going to achieve; he almost inspired me to pack and head right back home! By now I had been well grounded to look at challenges as an opportunity, so I was more determined to succeed. Of course, later we developed a mutual respect and I hold him in great respect today.

"In those days, an Indian selling software services to the Americans was a matter to be laughed at. After all, we had no experience or credentials to talk of. We continued to knock at doors hoping for the lucky break! The office was a one-man army: I typed letters, sent faxes and sometimes was even the delivery boy.

"It was very tough, but somewhere deep down I believed, as my many colleagues did, that we were not building a mere company but an industry that was a dream worth working towards.

"The challenges were on several fronts simultaneously – scarce and difficult US customers, bosses that were tough, the difficulties of dealing with the Indian government and its regulatory environment. To get a computer involved processing an import license. Looking back, we really went to the US to seek business because India and the Indian government were not yet ready then."

He was later able to share the insights he gained for the benefit of others:

"The US became our main business partner and a learning destination. We grew our operations across the East and West Coast years ago and I was later to visit, as their mentor and coach, the many regional managers posted there. In a foreign land and new culture, they were reliving my early experience. We made cold calls then and just imagine an Indian in a foreign car that he had just learnt to drive, in an unfamiliar city, on foreign roads with their rules and regulations, going to meet clients who were likely to slam the door on you.

"Not a very exciting prospect, but it brought its amusing moments. My advice to the managers was to recce the place to familiarize themselves the previous day before customer calls, so that there would be smooth sailing on the day of reckoning. Far from smooth sailing, many times this led to some rough waters. I remember the time in Chicago when the relationship manager took me to a location, supposedly the customer's office, except there was no building, and promptly declaring that he was certain it was there yesterday. Then the times at airports where we spent hours because the relationship manager had forgotten where he had parked the car. Or another time when typical Indian bravado got the better of him to drive right through a red light."

With such diverse experiences, some gained through adversity, the Tatas grew a strong culture that has evolved with the times, providing direction to the TCS team over the years. Ramadorai says:

"The Tata culture is phenomenal in terms of value system and ethics. No one teaches you or tells you but just practices it. It is within the DNA of the organization, you become a natural part of the value-added ethics.

"The opportunity for professional wellbeing is always considered most important. The idea is that if you build capabilities around good people that leads to wealth generation, monetary and intellectual, and gives you the opportunity to share with the society. The simple philosophy is that what comes from the people must go back to the people multiple times.

"In that sense the Tata culture is unique. Professionals, stakeholders, customers, and the community are all inter - connected. That is the ecosystem that has been created over the last 140 years."

Building on this solid foundation, Ramadorai set about creating his own blueprint for success:

"Every challenge has an opportunity hiding behind it. We learnt from the US and brought home the technology. This meant the need for more trained people. We joined hands with the Indian Institute of Technology, and we set up computer labs. It was the beginning of a whole support system for the industry to bloom.

"We were so busy building a company, an industry in India, while setting up global offshore models that when the IT boom of the 1990s happened we were more than happy to grab the opportunity. By then we were confident of the edge we and India had in the software services industry. That was our real growth spurt to become a global company. It was exciting to be in the middle of it all, with a young team and of course tremendous family support."

When Ramadorai took over at the helm of TCS in 1996, it had 5,000 employees. He steered the company to pole position, more than multiplying his workforce by 30 times. He recalls:

"Our core business in the past was 95 percent constituted of IT systems – application, development, maintenance, and transformation. That envelope extended to infrastructure services, business process outsourcing (BPO) and knowledge process outsourcing (KPO), consulting products, and intellectual assets. We leveraged this through our own R&D and our partnerships with third parties and academic institutions.

"This was gradually extended beyond Indian shores, beyond delivering out of India, into a global delivery model."

Turning Point

TCS was formed in 1968 to automate the operations of various Tata companies, so the small team of approximately 10 members started with menial tasks such as preparing punch cards. The leadership of Ramadorai and his top team has resulted in this same company's march to dominate global software services.

Realizing the need to grow organically, Ramadorai put together an ambitious plan in 2004 to raise capital by listing TCS on the Bombay Stock Exchange and by doing so making it one of the largest companies in India by market capitalization. Years after the mega-successful share issue, he mentions in hindsight:

"I was actually beginning to enjoy being in the driving seat when the IPO happened. Today, friends like you, the shareholders drive me. My bankers talk to me in a new football jargon of tackle, offense and defense. Mergers and acquisitions talk has become my staple food and life has become an ending story of 'quarter se quarter tak' [QSQT, an Indian acronym meaning a focus on quarterly results], from reducing fat to improving PAT, gaps in our competency to market cap, from past performance to future prediction."

Despite the onerous responsibilities that come with such a public share offering, Ramadorai continued looking at ways to make TCS bigger and better, As a result of careful analysis, he realized that the lion's share of revenues, approximately 95 percent, was the result of repeat business. While most of his competitors would have taken comfort in the simple fact that they had garnered a sense of loyalty from their clients, Ramadorai decided to turn the organization on its head, and ordered a restructuring in 2008 to focus on winning new, virgin business. This showed his determination to expand beyond his comfort zone to address missed opportunities.

Other than this obvious ambition, the new model also provided fresh opportunities for leadership growth at all levels and was widely hailed as a vital step in developing the next generation of leaders. Ramadorai says:

"We have made investments to diversify our revenues and grow in new markets, to develop new services and solutions, and build new delivery centers globally. These investments are already beginning to pay dividends. The above-average revenue growth from our emerging markets is helping to accelerate overall company growth."

In terms of the company's geographical spread, the UK added over $1 billion in revenue and the rest of Europe contributed over $500 million, while the revenue from the US has stayed at about 50 percent. Emerging markets, including Asia Pacific, Latin America, India and West Asia, and Africa, comprise almost $1 billion or about 20 percent of company revenue.

The third strand, which was an extension of the need to diversify revenues, was to set a challenge in countries like the UK to look at untapped opportunities in the lucrative public sector. With companies like BT, IBM, Capita, Accenture, and EDS firmly entrenched in the procurement process, opportunities to flourish seemed few. By investing in establishing an accomplished team comprising senior personnel who previously worked at those companies, TCS sought to meet the mindset of decision makers in Whitehall by utilizing the same methods as the incumbent operators had been using to win deals.

Knowing the contempt with which these companies were held by the taxpayer, due to massive failures in ambitious IT projects such as with the National Health Service, TCS rolled out a clever campaign using an integrated PR and government relations strategy. This resulted in its becoming an acceptable choice to deliver large-scale transformational IT projects in the UK, as it was in many parts of the world already. As a result of the focus on new business, in the face of competition from BT and IBM, TCS succeeded in bagging a deal to provide a new system that underpins the payment and enforcement of child maintenance, worth over £50 million in fees. Hot on the heels of that contract win, it was selected for a transformational deal with Cardiff City Council, thought to be worth £150 million over 15 years.

Interestingly, quite early on TCS mitigated the huge risk of negative coverage emanating from winning such high-profile public-sector contracts by highlighting that it is a responsible employer, leveraging the fact that the Tata group has deep roots in the UK and employs nearly 50,000 people across its diverse businesses. TCS also sought to clarify that just because the company hap pened to be Indian, that did not mean that it would offshore more jobs than any of the other Western suppliers. The strategy worked and the deal was welcomed in all quarters, at which point a huge sigh of relief could be heard in the boardrooms of the Indian out-sourcing fraternity. Ramadorai's push for new business is credited with opening the floodgates for other major Indian IT firms to gain business in the UK.

Key Strategy

Given the importance of the banking and financial services sector to developed economies, Ramadorai broke the mold in 2006 by acquiring the life and pensions business of Pearl Assurance (almost four million insurance policies), a leading insurer in the UK. In return for acquiring its assets and 950 employees, TCS netted a revenue boost worth $847 million over 12 years. Ramadorai said at the time:

> "The deal will help us emerge as a significant player in the life assurance and pensions administration services and help us continue our strong growth momentum."

TCS later rebranded this operation under the Diligenta banner, and won other deals to administer old life insurance and pension policies, from companies like Sun Life Financial of Canada.

Given its increased profile in the UK, TCS realized the need to sharpen up its communication and outreach. By doing so it has been able to build a trusted brand that seems to escape the clutches of the right-wing press, who love to write stories about jobs being lost to foreigners. This engagement stood the group in good stead in major acquisitions such as Corus and subsequently

Jaguar and Land Rover, where the trade unions actually endorsed the Tata bid on the basis of its being a good employer.

Likewise, in 2008 TCS struck gold with a groundbreaking agreement with Citigroup, a well-known global financial services company. It acquired all of Citi's interest in Citigroup Global Services Limited (CGSL), an India-based captive business processing outsourcing arm, for a cash consideration of approximately $505 million. CGSL has more than 12,000 employees located in India and expected to generate revenues of approximately $278 million in 2008. In addition to the sale, Citi signed an agreement for TCS to provide, through CGSL, BPO services to Citi and its affiliates for an aggregate amount of US$2.5 billion over 9.5 years. The deal built on an existing relationship between Citi and TCS whereby TCS provided application development, infrastructure support, helpdesk, and other process outsourcing services. The acquisition vastly broadened TCS's portfolio of end-to-end IT and BPO services in the global banking and financial services sector. Ramadorai said at the time:

> "This is a landmark acquisition for TCS, helping us not only acquire new capabilities in the banking domain but also underscoring the importance of our long-term, sustainable relationships with our large customers, including Citi. This transaction will complement our domain expertise and bring new capabilities to TCS that will help drive growth going forward."

In the course of these innovative deals, the company has kept a firm handle on the shaky economic conditions to tide it through the downturn. Ramadorai comments:

> "The market is going through a downturn and we have to exercise cautious optimism. There will be short-term delays, some decision making will be slow, but that does not mean we will shed our long-term partners. Every slowdown is fol-

lowed by a bounceback as the market strengthens. There are still plenty of possibilities in the IT world. We have to understand the complexities and apply them quickly with single-minded focus. The world now knows that Tata as a brand can be trusted."

In early 2009 a multimillion-dollar accounting fraud at Satyam Computer Services hit the headlines and threatened to strike a permanent dent in the world's confidence in the Indian IT sector, Ramadorai led the debate among his peers by articulating what the sector could do better:

"The industry has to step up to communicate a lot more effectively. It has to... keep saying and reinforcing that India is a great place to invest because of its potential and intellectual capacity."

Indian Perspective

The strength of a home-grown institution like TCS lies in its unflinching confidence in the product it has to offer. TCS may not yet have the reach of a company like IBM, but it is well placed to get there. And the crucial factor will be its Indian heritage:

"Indians tend to be a lot more inclusive, engaging, and hands-on to make globalization happen. We know we are coming from behind to catch up with the world. But we have the passion to make a difference. We believe in buying people over through our work rather than aggressive pushing. The management style is very much by example, by engaging, empowerment, and treating everybody as a true professional. We have always been very willing to learn quickly and are very mobile. We will give opportunity a shot."

That is the key reason most of the entry-level workforce are hired from India. Ramadorai explains:

> "India has the biggest raw material of entry-level professionals who can be trained very quickly and deployed very quickly. We are working on applying this phenomenon globally. European and American professionals come with a very multifaceted learning background and bring tremendous ability to manage large projects. We are working on combining these two aspects and training the Indians into these capabilities."

Another contributory factor in Ramadorai's success with TCS is the mentality with which all Tata companies are run. We know that Indians place a lot of value on the family unit, so it shouldn't come as a surprise that the Tata group functions in the same way. The group is cash rich, but each company is responsible for its own destiny. The only exception is when things become unstuck as they did with Jaguar Land Rover, when every member of the family pitches in to shoulder the load. Even with acquisitions, each company acquired is integrated into the Tata group, so that it benefits from the Tata way.

Ramadorai believes that this very Indian approach has also won over the critics of outsourcing:

> "Jobs being taken away will always be an election issue in the US, but most of it is not based on hard facts or data. At the end of the day, businesses will do what is best for them on a value-creation basis.
>
> "Our development center in Cincinnati is an example of creating centers of excellence that attract a massive local workforce. TCS has a fundamental belief in globalization of talent, be it US, Canada, Latin America, China, or India."

With people at the center of the business model, all employees on overseas projects receive country-specific cross-cultural training.

This improves their effectiveness in the workplace and helps them integrate more seamlessly into foreign climes. Likewise, TCS has also started offering its clients the option of training programs that make them aware of certain cultural nuances. We're not talking only about cultural training focused on India or Indians – as TCS employs people from virtually every country, it needs to offer this service to ensure that everyone, clients and employees, are singing from the same hymn sheet. Through education, it mitigates the risks related to stereotypes and other prejudices that may be to the detriment of its business.

Charity

In 2006, Ramadorai was awarded the Padma Bhushan, one of India's highest civilian honors. Beyond his contributions to the IT world, he has touched the lives of millions through his own brand of corporate social responsibility. He explains:

"I see it as corporate sustainability more than just responsibility. Basically the interests of all the stakeholders must come naturally, wherever you are in the world. Community and stakeholder wellbeing is the basic, be it through employees' extended family/spouses or through non-governmental organizations. Community initiatives, public–private partnerships should be geared towards the sole purpose of touching people in some form or other.

"I focus on education, health, setting up things like child line web portals, web health centers, national rural employment guarantee schemes and emergency support during natural disasters. All of this must come naturally in the corporate world if we are to sustain our growth."

This goal for sustainability extends to concerns for the climate:

"It is a big worry and we constantly try and put in programs as part of our corporate social responsibility to ensure we can be carbon neutral, cut down travel where it is not necessary, and use videoconferencing."

In 2005, when Hurricane Katrina was raging in the southern states of the US, TCS swung into action within days to work jointly with public agencies to design, develop, and deploy Mississippi's self-service Disaster Unemployment Assistance System. This enabled those who had lost their homes, businesses, and livelihoods to file for unemployment and other emergency funds. It is this level of commitment to local communities that TCS has built into its DNA.

In the UK, TCS has also been awarded the coveted Gold status on Business in the Community's corporate responsibility index. BCS is part of The Prince's Charities and focuses on improving the positive impact of companies on society.

All of this shouldn't really be a surprise, given that the founders of the Tata group bequeathed most of their personal wealth to the many trusts they created for the greater good of India and its people. Today, the Tata trusts control 65.8 percent of the shares of Tata Sons, the group's holding company. The wealth that accrues from this asset supports an assortment of causes, institutions, and individuals in a wide variety of areas.

Among his professional achievements that have brought many accolades, it is Ramadorai's unwavering commitment to social causes, community projects, and educational institutions that endears him to his peers and colleagues.

China

His foresight in dealing with macro issues earned Ramadorai the unusual role of IT adviser to Qingdao City in China. He comments:

"I see China as an opportunity because of its high domestic demand. You have to build patience, as doing business there is not easy. But the incremental growth and long-term sustainability are worth the wait. Comparatively India is in the early stages and gradually scaling it up.

"The ease with which one can set up a 'wholly owned foreign enterprise' in China in just three to four months is amazing. They are very clear in their aim – they want to be different. They also want to develop local talent and manpower to make it big at global levels."

With the benefit of his new assignment, Ramadorai is busy spotting opportunities for TCS in China.

Future Proofing

Having achieved huge success, Ramadorai retired from executive control in October 2009 in line with Tata policy. He says proudly:

"Even after I retire, Tata will be my first and only priority. The most satisfying feeling is to leave an institution where I began as a start-up company when it has a global standing. The brand is recognized and it has inherent strengths that will ensure that it moves to the next level of growth and vision without the person responsible being there in person. The enablers for success are not dependent on one person. They are ingrained in its very being."

Given such loyalty, it came as no surprise when Ratan Tata created the new position of Vice-Chairman for Ramadorai. After all, who would want so many years of experience and success to walk away?

Family

With his life focused around the Tata Group, Ramadorai has hardly taken any time out for a holiday or a break with his family. He recalls one incident:

"On the personal front, the best thing in my life – my son Tarun – brought great joy. I'm sure he found my frequent absences from home objectionable, for I'm told he confronted Kohli one day asking him why he made me work so hard. Today we share a wonderful friendship. In those days there were no crèches, we took our kids along everywhere, through all the travel and parties, but we felt the need for a support system and the idea finally took form recently, our initiative called Maitree, which is run by the spouses of TCS employees and engages TCS's extended family in a variety of ways."

His biggest role model after Mahatma Gandhi is Tata Group scion Ratan Tata:

"If there is one person after my parents and Gandhi that I look up to, it is Ratan Tata for his phenomenal vision. He believes in empowerment and building strong young teams. No problem is difficult, only challenging. His entire value system and ethics are based on a deep consideration for human beings."

This humility extends to Ramadorai's own life, where he sees wealth as something to be shared and distributed. He and his wife Mala and son Tarun share a love for their holiday home in the lush hill station of Khandala, near Mumbai. His only extravagance is an obsession with new-fangled gadgets:

"I love gadgets. I need to have the latest iPod and attach-ments because I love North Indian and Carnatic classical music on long walks. I do try and find time to follow sports and enjoy cricket a lot. I have been supporting the Mumbai and Chennai Indian Premier League teams, though my loyalty lies more with Mumbai."

Ramadorai is a man committed to work. I am left with no doubt that he would have given all he had to whichever company he joined. He may not technically be an entrepreneur, but he has very successfully developed an entrepreneurial culture in TCS, which has propelled it to a global powerhouse employing over 130,000 people and raking in over $5.7 billion in revenues.

When we look at hard facts, established companies like IBM and Fujitsu Siemens command huge respect for delivering software services to many of the world's companies, but what Ramadorai has achieved is no less. Despite the burdensome duties of being a publicly listed company, Ramadorai's focus on the next wave of services has delivered huge returns to shareholders, providing TCS with a market capitalization of $11.6 billion that is slowly catching up with contenders like Accenture. Ramadorai's legacy will rank as highly as some of India's most successful leaders.

Remembering his journey, which started in an era in which India was just getting used to being an independent country and Indian firms didn't enjoy anywhere near the kind of status they do today, any lesser being would easily have buckled under such huge pressures and change. In spite of adversity, Ramadorai rose to the occasion. As a conclusion, he remarks:

"And by the way, now that I am older and wiser I know the hidden message my kite had for me. I've learnt never to be afraid of opposition. Remember, a kite rises against, and not with, the wind."

Kishore Lulla

- CEO of Eros International, India's largest distributor of films and entertainment.
- Three decades of market leadership in creating a platform for Indian cinema. Eros operates in over 50 countries and has a turnover of $150 million.
- Dreams of consolidating the fragmented Indian film industry to take on the global might of Hollywood and make India an entertainment superpower.
- With a film catalog of 2,000 titles and 5,000 music videos, passionate about using YouTube and other new-media opportunities to reach a larger global audience.
- Apart from his movies, loves cars and drives around London in an Aston Martin, a Bentley, and a Range Rover.

Mr. Bollywood

He may not have a billion-dollar turnover like the others in this book; he doesn't even have many offices or factories to boast of; and he definitely hasn't been recognized by the Indian or any other government for his achievements. Nevertheless, the penetration of Indian entertainment abroad is down to Kishore Lulla and his company, Eros International.

I was reminded how popular Indian movies are on my honeymoon. My wife and I decided to find our bearings in Bali by taking a stroll near our hotel. At any shop or street stall, the owner would, as if on autopilot, enquire whether we were from India and quickly follow up by saying that Tejal looked like Sridevi, a popular yesteryear actress, and I resembled Amitabh Bachchan, the most iconic actor in the Indian film industry. As much as I'd like to believe this is the case, others have experienced much the same elsewhere, and what is evident is the sheer popularity of Bollywood films in far-flung corners of the planet.

Very little gives away the true vocation of the man responsible for getting the world to sit up and take notice of the Indian film industry. Unassuming, media shy, and soft-spoken, Lulla has been forced out of his hiding place behind the cameras as Bollywood races ahead on the fast track of global domination. He is Chief Executive of Eros International, an AIM-listed company with a current market value of $325 million and is well on his way to branding his company as the first true Indian film studio along the lines of Hollywood.

His winning mantra is a simple one: "Cash is king but content is the emperor." The content is the vast array of over 1,000 romantic, action, or dramatic weepies that the Indian film industry churns out every year. This is not only double the number coming from the world's biggest film producers in Los Angeles, Bollywood movies claim an audience of over four billion people. The Indian industry is expected to be worth a whopping $50 billion by 2015 and Lulla knows that Eros is the key to hitting that magical figure. He says:

> "Everybody says you must make your dream come true, but I say you must make your wish come true. I wish that Bollywood films would gross worldwide the same as Hollywood and hit the billion-dollar mark. That has been my wish for the last 10–15 years and I think we are nearly there. You have to have an intuition about these things. It will be the least expected film that will hit the mark."

He reckons Bollywood is where Hollywood was in the 1930s and 1940s, but will take only a decade to catch up with its prime rival. This mission of world domination relying on the soft power of Indian films may sound overly ambitious, but he has done the math. He explains:

> "My take is that there are 1.1 billion people in India and 400 million South Asians living outside India with a disposable income. There are 13,000 screens in India and 400 multiplexes. Malls are being made and townships being created on a daily basis. We sold 3.9 billion tickets in 2007 in India alone. Hollywood sold 3.1 billion in comparison. Ticket prices are around $1–2 and will rise to $3–4. For this reason, in the next five years the same film will gross $100 million at the box office in the first week. At the moment when the entire world watches, a Hollywood film grosses $1 million. That will start to happen in India alone. That is what I mean when I say Bollywood is catching up."

Global Vision

It is this faith in the content he has to offer that drives Lulla's global strategy. Eros started out as a purely intellectual property rights business dedicated to acquiring the rights to movies and exploiting the copyright in various markets across the world. Over the years, there has been a conscious shift toward creating a traditional studio model, which includes making movies, marketing and distributing them, and, ultimately, pocketing the profits. Lulla reiterates:

"The future, as I see it, is cross-pollination between Bollywood and Hollywood. I have tremendous respect for Hollywood studios, but we are trying to do what they did in 90 years in just 10 years. India is going global. Its food has gone global, its fashion has gone global and its movies will go global."

The cross-pollination has already begun. In 2008, Eros finalized a deal with Sony that will see the global media powerhouse invest £30 million in four Eros films that have the potential to be distributed to Western audiences. This was followed by another big-fish pact with Hollywood giant Lionsgate, which will gain a wider American market for Eros films while adding Lionsgate films to the Eros library to exploit a whole new Indian market. Lulla explains:

"Sony brings expertise in marketing, putting in their money and creative know-how. They know how a film should be written and positioned to an audience outside the South Asian diaspora and we already know how to position it within. So the public is getting better and better movies and for Eros it means a better bottom line, more money. They are sharing the risk with us. Lionsgate comes with 15,000 DVD titles, which we can sell in India. That again means more choice for the consumer.

"We have a deal with Google, which uses new media to reach out to viewers on online channels such as YouTube. It has more than 50 million viewers and is a great marketing tool for us where we post videos and ads of films, plus make money on it.

"We launched a video-on-demand subscription with Comcast Corp and Movielink in the US to provide our films to the four million South Asians there. We are available on Amazon, on BskyB... any media format and Eros is there."

In these tie-ups across different countries and formats, there is a very clear-cut focus on India. While Lulla is happy to model himself on Warner Bros or Disney, he has no plans to invest in Hollywood just yet. He is certain that India is where Eros's growth market lies, although he also has a keen eye on Indonesia, Malaysia, Thailand, Germany, Poland, Russia, and China. He says:

"All these countries consume Hollywood movies in a dubbed environment. But in the last 20 years we have seen them embracing Bollywood in a big way because it brings a breath of fresh air. It gives them music, it gives them family values, something different from Hollywood. And we have seen a breakout success of many films into these markets.

"We want to learn from Hollywood studios. Our role model has been the five big studios so we have been trying to incorporate a little bit of Sony, a little bit of Warner, a little bit of Disney, Newscorp, and Fox. It also means seeing what mistakes they have made in the last 100 years and trying not to make them.

"But Hollywood is a dangerous area to go into in terms of investment. I do not want to play that volatile game. I am sitting on a goldmine market, which is India. There will be major growth in India in the next five years. PricewaterhouseCoopers has predicted the market will grow at 18 percent a year. Hollywood's growth has plateaued out in the last five years."

This unique synergy has worked wonders for Eros. Around 50 percent of its profits come from India. Its films are dubbed into 27 foreign languages, a figure that is continually on the rise as new markets get attracted to the song-and-dance fare on offer. Only 4–5 percent of its revenues come from the American market.

Eros boasts an overseas growth rate of 25 percent across all formats. Television syndication and digital and new ancillary rights have registered a 200 percent hike in profits in six months.

When each new market and country starts watching Bollywood films, it brings innumerable opportunities for Eros. Slowly but surely, Eros leverages its huge existing catalog of thousands of films to earn its fortune.

Background

However, there was a time when things were not all glitz and glamor in this business. Eros was set up by Kishore's father, Arjan Lulla, in 1977 when he spotted a gap in the market. There were several million people of South Asian origin living outside the country of their birth and most of them were understandably nostalgic about the melodramatic stories offered by Bollywood, but had no access to them in a pre-internet world.

Arjan started distributing Indian movies the old-fashioned way, in steel tins, to the UK and the US and to less obvious places like the UAE and Israel. Kishore explains:

> "Dad started the company with a view to exploit Indian content worldwide. He was into financing some movies and selling their rights. That's the time I told him instead of selling the rights, let's exploit them by holding the IPR rights ourselves."

By holding on to the rights to films, Kishore realized that they could use these to gain a foothold in countries to which Indians had migrated. He says:

"Globalization was not heard of back then. I had a dream that one day Bollywood would go global and everybody will embrace Bollywood. I am proud to say that in 30 years of this journey, we had to face a lot of hardships in reaching audiences across the globe, many difficulties in our path, but everybody has embraced Bollywood today."

The young starry-eyed law graduate convinced his father to open offices across the world rather than depending on local agents, As a result, today Eros operates in 50 different countries, and has offices ranging from Malaysia to the Fiji Islands to the Isle of Man. Kishore's own wanderlust took him around the Middle East before he decided to set up base in London in 1980. The Eros catalog was born at its UK base with popular blockbuster *Ghulami*. He reminisces:

"It was a time of a lot of ups and downs. Opening up offices abroad and making money on the movies was definitely an up. When you are young it is also all about making money. It was great to work with different filmmakers, open up different markets. But the biggest downer was that a lot of people used to look down on Bollywood. It was perceived as not a good industry to be in, and rightly so because there were many unwanted elements in Bollywood like the casting couch. You couldn't help but feel low that you are in such an industry. However, we were no less than any other industrialists and today we demand the same respect because we are churning out billions of dollars. It is all about the money at the end of the day, how much profit you generate."

The film industry had a dark underbelly in the form of the Indian mafia, dubbed the Mumbai underworld. It had turned the filmmaking business into the biggest money-laundering operation in Asia. Criminally earned cash from drugs and the illegal arms trade was plowed into film production and laundered money was regained at the box office. There are plenty of stories of actors, producers, and underworld bosses working in tandem with each other, even socializing on the party circuit in Mumbai.

The Indian government's decision to give films the much-needed "industry" status in 2002 helped clean up the mess. Lulla acknowledges the seedy side of his field as the main reason he kept out of the Indian market for nearly 25 years:

> "It was similar to the 1930s and 1940s Hollywood mobs. It had unfortunately arisen because the government never supported it as an industry. So when producers made films they never got money from banks or corporates like us. That's the reason Eros never operated in India until 2005. The India office was just a film acquisition center. Back then we had to be really careful. Once industry status was granted, it is now totally clean. I can safely say there is no underworld element. There is enough money around. It was all down to money, a way of whitewashing the system."

Business

What set Eros apart was not just that it managed to stay clean during the bad old days, but also that its boss shared a special rapport with every big player in the film industry. These bonds come in handy today when many of the newcomers have turned into superstars, capable of churning out a million dollars at the box office by simply attaching their names to a film.

In most cases, Lulla fixes his costs with long-term talent contracts for a slate of 60 movies stretching over a period of three years. He explains:

> "Everyone knows content should be king. In Hollywood, the screenplay drives the director and the director drives the actor. In India, there is still too much star power. The stars

drive the director and the director drives the screenwriter. Exactly what happened in Hollywood in the 1980s will happen in Bollywood. If the stars want to get paid too much, the industry will simply look elsewhere."

It is no mean feat to keep all these big stars and their even bigger egos in check. Nevertheless, it comes naturally to Lulla, who has not only risen alongside some of them but also helped them get where they are on a global platform.

His biggest ally and unique selling point remains Shah Rukh Khan, often referred to as the Brad Pitt of India for his sheer charisma and pulling power at the box office. The success of one of Eros's highest-grossing films, *Om Shanti Om*, was down to King Khan. But to Lulla he remains an old friend, as do any of the other biggies such as Amitabh Bachchan or Hrithik Roshan. Lulla says:

"See, they are big today but we have grown together. Shah Rukh used to earn Rs 10 lakhs 10 years ago, when I was making Rs 5 lakhs on a movie. Before he was a star, he used to come over my place. We worked hard together on early films like *Baazigar*. So for me Shah Rukh may become the biggest star of the world, but even today he will come to my place for dinner. That is the kind of relationship you build, it is not based on your market capitalization or how successful you are. So we don't have egos, we just do what's right."

And that seems to have worked like a charm for Eros. It now has a slice of film production that complements its distribution network. It has ownership of all world rights, with platforms on cable, satellite, and digital channels in India and across the world.

Eros also has part ownership of a popular television channel, B4U. It has rights to distribute thousands of Hollywood movies in India and emerging markets across Southeast Asia. A lot of its profits come from music soundtracks, extremely popular among

Bollywood fans the world over. And the newest source of revenue is pouring in from its dubbed films. Lulla comments:

> "We are a one-stop shop for content. Our studio model means we own content, distribute it across the globe in all formats, and also commission maybe one a year. We buy films from producers on different terms, we can own it out-right or have a share with him. But we own the sole distri-bution rights across all formats, including theater, DVD, VHS, TV, satellite, internet, you name it. Anywhere on the planet that you watch that film, that deal has been syndi-cated by Eros."

Turning Point

This sense of pride is not misplaced from the man who turned Eros into the world's first Bollywood public limited company. Its listing on London's Alternative Investment Market in 2006 effort-lessly raised $100 million to fund the company's expansion plans. Lulla says:

> "It gave respectability to the Indian film industry, bringing it at par with Hollywood. The last few years have really been about enjoying the game because denomination values have become huge. Everybody says that Bollywood in the next 10 years will be a $50–100 billion industry. If you are a major player in that industry, it is not only a matter of pride but also proves that whatever we believed in 30 years ago has come true. We didn't lose hope, didn't lose our interest through all the hiccups."

And there were many. The biggest threat to the industry came from the invention of the video in the 1980s. Doomsday predic-tions claimed that it was the end of the theater-going era of cinema

149

and big box office revenues. But in hindsight, Lulla is confident that movie theaters will never die out. He explains:

"A movie's first home is the theater, that is where you want to enjoy it. There will be a lot of formats coming up, definitely – like DVD, Blu-ray, and mobile phones. But you can still not enjoy a film like you can in a theater. Every aspect has its value, but 30–40 percent of the revenue from a movie comes from its box office collections.

"The consumer will always be king in terms of how he wants to watch content – in the theater, on DVD, TV, pay-per-view, or on the iPod. If we restrict how content is watched, then we are hitting our own bottom line. So Eros is embracing all technologies as long as it makes commercial sense. Hence we are at the forefront of Indian cinema.

"The credit crunch is impacting everyone. In this atmosphere of gloom, the movie-making industry remains recession proof because families can cut down on holidays, going out to restaurants, but they still need entertainment. When things are gloomy, you go out and buy a cinema ticket and maybe opt for a cheaper meal. Escapist and larger-than-life films have always proved big grossers during wars and recession."

Indian Perspective

Nevertheless, it is not just escapist cinema that Eros is interested in. Over the years, Lulla has made a conscious effort to position himself where he can call the shots on the kind of films his company will co-produce and distribute. His strong karmic beliefs make him averse to any films that give out the wrong message. As a studio, his goal is to be seen as on a par with the likes of Disney, popular for its family-oriented, wholesome entertainment. He explains:

"Believe in yourself, believe in your karma. If there is some good I can do to the world by teaching them Hindu culture, that is what I would like Hollywood to learn from Bollywood. The law of karma is what goes around, comes around. Nothing is by coincidence. It is all cause and effect. You must take responsibility for what you are today and whatever happens to you.

"At Eros, we will never support a film that glorifies violence in any way. We will not make money on someone's tragedy or by hurting feelings. Any film that is in production at the moment and every script has gone through me. We will never venture into a film that gives out a bad social message. We cannot put our name to a sex movie or drugs or terrorism or an anti-family film, no matter how much money it may make. I feel very socially responsible."

This strong belief in his product has strengthened over the years, through a few mistakes along the way. Lulla does regret being associated with J P Dutta's war film *Border* in 1997, a smash hit at the box office but widely discredited for its strong anti-Pakistan rhetoric. He says:

"Maybe I would not do it today. We did it back then because we were not yet thinking like a studio. It was all about the bottom line. When you are a player in a small industry, you want to get hold of every decent product that works. But now there is not a single script that will go against our core beliefs."

Filmmaking is clearly beyond a mere business proposition for Lulla. He may be driven by the bottom line in most cases, but he has a strong sense of pride in the brand that is Bollywood:

"We don't have to brand ourselves. Bollywood is a well-known brand today. Everything in this industry is a new day, unlike any other industry. It's a very creative thing, every day brings a new challenge like how best to make and market a certain movie. Over the next few years, creativity will rule the world. Films are very powerful, they can change opinions and views.

"Our films like *Baghban* and *Munnabhai* changed views on violence and family values. I am certain they would have converted a lot of people. Our films are made from the soul and appeal to the soul. When you go through scripts, you can't really pick a winner. It is all God's doing and a lot of luck factor. One in every five films will be a hit. No one can claim to pick only hits. You go by your intuition and sixth sense and hope for the best. No human can take credit for that.

"My intuition tells me a Bollywood film will soon do what *Crouching Tiger, Hidden Dragon* did by capturing the world's imagination and crossing the billion-dollar mark as a Chinese film. A film that can make money and give a message, that for me is a successful film. Ultimately a film is as successful as the box office because it shows that people have loved it. Sometimes it is nice to have critical acclaim as well, but if I am putting up the public's money as a listed company, the box office becomes even more important."

And he is confident of box office domination in the wake of the international success story of *Slumdog Millionaire*. The Danny Boyle-directed British film set in India and made using a mix of Indian and international cast and crew marked a new era for the Indian film industry that Eros is all set to capitalize on. Lulla is planning a whole new division within his company dedicated to developing this fresh talent. Clearly excited about this wider cinematic horizon, he says:

"It is an Indian movie, with the slums as a backdrop... it is totally Indian, just made by Danny Boyle. It was made within $5–10 million and will gross at least $100 million. It will open the floodgates for Indian movies. There are many talented makers in India who can make such a movie with $2–3 million. *Slumdog* will open up the market. I am planning a new label in Eros, which will be concentrating on movies like this – Indian with a foreign director. The new division will hunt for and nurture this new talent. We already have the machinery and distribution outfit to put it out."

However, the buzzword remains content and he stresses that the basic element of filmmaking will always stay the same:

"Look at the films we were producing 10 years ago and look at them now. There is a vast difference in terms of technology and packaging. But they all still make you laugh and cry. Indians are very loud people anyway. We express our emotions loudly and we are not ashamed of it."

Charity

This emotional side to Lulla extends to a strong impulse to share his profits with the world at large. Someone who counts Microsoft founder Bill Gates as his role model, Lulla clearly falls into the category of entrepreneurs who believe in wealth distribution as much as wealth creation. He says:

"Bill Gates made all that money and gave it away for a good cause. That is the hard part, you can make the money and sustain it but to then give it away... if everyone can do that, the world would be a beautiful place. That is the reason 50 percent of whatever we make goes straight to our foundation, whatever the amount I may earn. There is nothing like enough money for human beings, so this system is an automatic adjustment."

That is not the only message he has taken from Microsoft. At a more practical level, he has adopted the Gates approach to tackling threats to the business such as film piracy:

> "Piracy is a killer. But we have decided to take the Microsoft model. They let piracy happen, let people get used to their product, and then started implementing the licenses and taking action. I think for a business to grow, sometimes you have to overlook these things. We want audiences to get used to our product, let them get hooked. What is the point of controlling piracy if there is no demand for the product?"

A unique balance between spiritualism and pragmatism seems to govern most aspects of his film business:

> "If something really bad happens, I try and look at it in the best possible way. I feel you are God's child and God will not put you in a situation that is bad for you. That is why I don't care if people say negative things. It is reflected back on them."

Future Proofing

Its strong focus on delivery is the main factor behind Eros being the market leader in its field. Lulla sees Asia as the hub of film-making in the coming years and knows he is ready to take advantage of that surge. He predicts:

> "I see an amalgamation of the Asian film industry and Hollywood. The Korean film industry is doing really well. Who knows, but the next Pokemon character could be from India instead of Japan. Hollywood rules about 70 percent of the whole global entertainment industry and 30 percent is for the rest of the world. That equation will change in the next 5–10 years.

"If somebody had said 30 years ago that the Japanese car industry would take over the American car industry, no one would have believed it. So I am confident it is going to happen in the next 10–20 years. Korea is coming out very strong with a lot of new creative ideas. The real competition will be between Korea, China, and Bollywood."

While some might be skeptical of the global winning power of Bollywood, Lulla feels he no longer needs to prove its power:

"We have got our movies everywhere. They are dubbed into 27 languages. Ask any Thai, Russian, or German, they know what Bollywood movies are, they sing our songs. It is reaching out to so many people with its unique music and culture. Indian stars like Shah Rukh Khan get mobbed by the locals in Berlin.

"Bollywood is truly global today. Every hit gives us a buzz, every flop makes us try and learn from our mistakes. There is not a single company with a 100 percent hit record. No one can get everything right."

Family

Eros may be run on a strong family ethos and its films may reflect family values, but Lulla is very clear about the need for professionalism in order to be recognized as a global film studio. "I can exit today if someone gives me the right price," he jokes, but he is clearly devoted to making the Eros success story even bigger:

"I want to concentrate on this business as over the next five years it will mature a lot. We own 24 percent of [Indian entertainment channel] B4U, which I feel could have done much better if it was under Eros management. However, at the moment we are not looking at expansion into broadcasting due to the credit crunch. The focus is mainly on consolidation of the business, but maybe one day we would like to integrate the whole business into a large media conglomerate."

Meanwhile, he does not see himself as indispensable to the business and insists that it is purely his hunches that are working for now. The business continues to rely heavily on the family element and Lulla's brother Sunil is in charge of India operations. Most of the other senior staff have been with Eros for some time, including COO Jyoti Deshpande and Vice-Chairman and President Vijay Ahuja.

Lulla's two daughters have the option of joining the business, but it is not a foregone conclusion. He explains:

"We Indians work from our heart, give it our best. Eros has the ethos of a family enterprise but the working is totally corporate. Evaluation of the company is important, transparency is important. Being a listed concern, we have to be totally compliant with disclosures. My daughters, if they are fit enough for any aspect of the business, are most welcome, but this is not a family dynasty so that it will be automatic. We have members of management who have been with us for almost 25 years and are in senior positions of authority."

But one area where his daughters do get the final say is in holiday plans. Be it St Tropez or Mumbai, holidays are a key bonding time for the Lulla family, away from their elegant home in the north London suburb of Totteridge. They also have a hand in how he looks:

"I leave my styling to my wife and daughters. There are the usual suspects – Dolce & Gabbana and Armani. But I largely like being in casuals. As a media company, we don't follow the suit and tie culture."

Compared with the other titans of Indian industry I interviewed, Lulla came across as exceptional and unique. I have seen him on the London circuit at parties and events, but one occasion summed up his dominance for me.

I was invited to attend the London première of a blockbuster film called *Om Shanti Om*. As is the format for such events, its stars were invited to say a few words to the august audience before the film started. When each of the stars spoke, whether it was the newly unveiled sex siren Deepika Padukone or model turned actor John Abraham, or even the King of Bollywood Shah Rukh Khan, they made huge references to their success being down to one man – Kishore Lulla.

If Bollywood is India's religion, Lulla is its god.

Tulsi R Tanti

■ Chairman of Suzlon Energy, the world's third largest supplier of wind turbines and other complete end-to-end wind power solutions.

■ Asia's largest wind turbine manufacturer, spread across 21 countries and five continents.

■ Recognized as one of *Time* magazine's "Heroes of the Environment" and by the United Nations Environment Program as a "Champion of the Earth" for his contribution to raising awareness and initiating action on global climate change.

■ A serial entrepreneur: Suzlon is his 17th enterprise. His journey began with a decision he was asked to make: would he prefer to manage his family's cinema halls or its cold storage facility? Guess which one he opted for?

The Climate Change Billionaire

Very few entrepreneurs can boast a billion-dollar enterprise built, quite literally, on air. That's why the Tanti story makes interesting reading.

Tulsi R Tanti sells windmills and is one of the biggest players in the field. He is the face of wind energy in India and is on his way to becoming a global market leader. The US is focused on securing its energy supply, the EU is showing strong support for tackling climate change, and the boom in Asia has resulted in a greater demand for electricity. Such factors bode well for Tanti and Suzlon Energy.

Referred to as "Tiger" by his friends for the aggression he shows in his business, Tanti has always dreamt big and matched his company's growth rate with his dreams. His wind turbine business has consistently grown at more than double the rate of the existing market.

His driving force is very simply what he describes as "common sense":

"Wind energy can, and will, play one of the most important roles in saving the world tomorrow, today. I drive my business as a cause, one where we power a greener tomorrow.

"We have a very clear vision, strategy, and plan. I can write down a 10-year balance sheet for you right now, Suzlon is that focused. I want to put the wind energy sector at a completely different level. It is my contribution to society. Low-cost energy is very important for the common people of the developing world. Alternative sources of energy are the reality of today. So while I make money, I want to take care of the environment at the same time."

Tanti is confident that the increasing oil and gas prices coupled with concerns about global warming will present him with an opportunity to grab a quarter of the global market for wind energy by 2015.

His company covers 21 countries on five continents. It was the first Indian company to export wind turbines to the US market back in 2003 and it now has manufacturing bases there besides India and China, Germany and Belgium.

Tanti is well known for changing the rules of the game. When other players were selling equipment, he went into the market with a full-service package and grabbed a 50 percent share of the Indian market in the process. Not far behind Al Gore when it comes to rattling off carbon facts, he proudly proclaims:

> "I can talk about global warming and climate change for 48 hours non-stop. Carbon concentration in the atmosphere was 280 parts per million at the start of industrialization and is now 387 ppm. It could touch 600 ppm by 2030 with the industrialization of India and China."

Tanti's concern goes beyond merely spelling out the facts, to actual solutions to tackle the problem. This practical approach has helped him take on the challenges thrown up by the credit crunch, which has driven up energy costs even further. But the answer to all our troubles, he believes, is (literally) blowing in the wind.

Global Vision

The Suzlon story began in 1995 with only 20 people. In just over a decade it has acquired epic proportions. The name Suzlon was born out of an amalgamation of the Gujarati words *suz-buz* (know-how) and *lon* (bank loan).

Now a company employing almost 15,000 people from 23 different nationalities, Suzlon has operations across America, Asia, Australia, and Europe, manufacturing units on three continents, sophisticated research and development capabilities and market leadership in Asia, and a joint rank of fourth with REpower Systems AG, with 12.3 percent global market share in 2008. Its management headquarters are located in Pune, India and its European and Latin American marketing headquarters are in Aarhus, Denmark, with a network of offices spanning Chicago, Beijing, Melbourne, and Mumbai.

In 2003, the company sold its first turbine in the US market. This was an important milestone in its ambitious global plans, as it was the first such export from Asia to a developed country. Tanti explains:

> "We were offering a very high-end technology. It was too early to capture Asia with it and the US was a natural choice. After India, it is now our largest market, followed closely by China.
>
> "The front end of the international organization was in Denmark, responsible for marketing because they have rich experience in producing turbines and exporting them around the world. I could see here is the right talent, so I established a management team and from there moved to the US, Europe, Brazil, Australia, China. I have consciously not transferred any Indian managers to any of these markets; we have taken the local experts and given a free hand to them. Each country's management team reports to the group management team, which is based in Pune. Each of these teams have a target for their market and the entire corporate team supports them."

In 2006 Tanti snapped up Belgium-based Hansen Transmissions International NV, the world's second largest wind energy and industrial gearbox manufacturers, for a whopping $565 million. The all-cash deal catapulted Suzlon into the big league as an integrated wind turbine maker. At a stroke, it got rid of its dependence on global players for supplying gearboxes. Tanti says:

> "We saw a very important opportunity. It was the most reliable gearbox manufacturer at the time. Once we acquired it, the target was set for the team to expand capacity from 2,700 MW to 6,000 MW in Belgium. Once that was completed, Hansen's total capacity including India and

China is on its way to becoming 14,300 MW, which is a growth of over five times in six years. Within 18 months of acquisition, Hansen was listed on the London stock market valued at $3 billion, which gave us further investment to expand capacity with full equity."

Strategic acquisitions around the world continued in 2007 with part of REpower, a German firm known for its technological prowess in the wind energy space globally. At the time, it was billed as India's third largest M&A deal, valued at $1.8 billion. Tanti says:

"REpower was a very high-tech and engineering-driven company. That is the essence of this business, to get the cream of the sector. It brings a very innovative approach to the team. Within the sector, REpower is way ahead. Their 5 MW and 6 MW turbines are already commercialized and selling in the market. Suzlon today owns a 90.72 percent stake in REpower."

The purchase of REpower, beating French nuclear energy giant Areva to the acquisition, enabled Suzlon to extend its presence in Europe and have a wider and stronger portfolio of products to capitalize on growing global demand at a faster rate. Nevertheless, the economic downturn hit the energy sector hard and Tanti was forced to reschedule his payments for the stake in REpower owned by Martifer, a Portuguese construction and energy company, which he has now completed.

Tanti says that by 2020 there will be only five to six global players in the industry, and to survive Suzlon needs to be big in the US, Europe, and Asia. His logic is that unlike in the US and Asia, where land is plentiful, in Europe he needs giant offshore wind turbines to produce electricity. REpower's 6 MW generator – double the power output of Suzlon's biggest turbine – is 100m tall and has a rotor diameter of 126m. It can only be serviced using a helicopter. Coupled with this technology and a cost base nearly

19 percent lower than the European company, Tanti claims that he can grow REpower's business fivefold within a short time.

The economic turmoil has not shaken his faith in the growth prospects of wind energy. In 2009, Suzlon entered the nascent Sri Lankan market with an order to deliver eight 1.25 MW turbines to the Kalpitiya region. Construction on the project is expected to be completed by 2010. The order is an important milestone for Suzlon as it is the first Sri Lankan wind project to feature megawatt-class turbines, and the first to be developed by a private company.

Suzlon is constructing Asia's largest wind park in Kutch, Gujarat, with a planned capacity of nearly 1,500 MW when completed. Future plans include exceeding it in size, to create an even larger wind farm in Inner Mongolia that will generate 1,650 MW of wind power. Tanti says:

"The key to our success will be leadership in technology. I am quite confident that in three years, we will be leaders in the market. We already have a 6 MW product that is a benchmark for others; the next step is to commercialize it and ensure that benefits are passed along to the end consumer. Our focus remains on innovation and technology.

"The demand is huge because oil prices are soaring. China alone plans to have an installed capacity of 100,000 MW – the entire world today has a total capacity of 120,000 MW as of 2008. We have to grow fast to cater to this demand.

"Today we are in 21 countries, we plan to be in another 20 plus countries in the next five years. We plan to grow at twice the industry rate of 20–25 percent."

Background

The 16-member Tanti family, including Tulsi, his three brothers, and the extended family, today own 53 percent of Suzlon. It has been a long journey from the Gujarati clan's origins in Rajkot, where they used to run a cold storage unit.

Tanti joined the family business in 1978 after graduating in commerce and mechanical engineering. His urge to sharpen his entrepreneurial skills led him to attend commerce classes in the day and engineering ones in the evening. He comments:

> "These two different kinds of knowledge have really helped me make a success of any business. One side of my brain can understand numbers and the other side understands technology. Integrate that to trigger value creation and you have the growth opportunity."

Once he was ready, his father presented him with two business options for taking the helm: the family's cold storage firm or its cinema halls. He took a day to decide that the former was his calling. Asked why, he simply says that there was more technology involved in the cold storage business, which meant higher growth potential. He adds:

> "Within one year, I had worked out the cost breakdown – where the revenue was coming from and where the money was going. The margin was somewhere around 10 percent and nearly 40 percent of the cost was taken up by electricity, as cold storage is run on air conditioning. I could see technological changes were required and within a year I had reduced the electricity bill by 40 percent, doubling the profit to 22 percent."

Within three years the family had decided to move base to Surat, the textile hub of India. They introduced a polyester microfilament yarn and upholstery fabrics, 90 percent of which were exported to the US market. Tanti introduced a range of technical innovations along with a number of new products, using very high-tech imports from Taiwan, Korea, and Japan. He developed a synthetic yarn for sarees and dress materials that mimicked real silk.

These experiments were completely different from the family business and gave him the chance to spread his wings. He is credited with setting up 17 companies around this time, dabbling in real estate and the stock market. He kept moving from one business to the other, transferring ownership or selling it lock, stock, and barrel. He says:

"From an entrepreneurial point of view, I can do anything. I can even run a hospital. Ultimately it's about how you deal with people and how you manage the stakeholder requirements. Industry is just a tool or medium. I like to move from one challenge to the next."

However, throughout this phase he found himself continually mulling over the high cost of energy. In 1994, he felt that was the biggest barrier to growth because every year the cost of electricity was on the rise. His profit margin was around 5 percent but the cost of energy added up to 40–50 percent.

He got into wind energy quite by accident while looking into various solutions to this problem. He recalls:

"From day one, the focus was energy, be it cold storage or textile. I would try out different types of boilers and power generators. Lot of continuous study was going into this. I realized that everything is dependent on fuel, gas, or oil. Why not find something that does not require fuel?

"That gave me the idea to use a windmill as the best solution. I purchased two and set them up in Gujarat. The power went to the electricity board and I got the credit for it in my factory. So I had hedged my power costs for 20 years.

"Then I got thinking, why do this just for one company? Why not the whole sector, then the whole country, and now the whole world? That has given me the drive. You can call it luck or anything, but it is this continuous effort to optimize on our energy reductions that has spurred me to go towards a renewable source like wind."

Between 1994 and 2000 he spent his time understanding the market. He soon became a niche player in the niche market of India, starting with one state and then expanding to eight. He then spent the last decade becoming the market leader in India.

Suzlon began modestly with a wind farm project in Gujarat with a capacity of just 3 MW; by 2008 it was supplying more than 7,000 MW the world over. It is today considered a truly home-grown Indian multinational.

Three of India's biggest entrepreneurial giants – Reliance, Tata, and Infosys – provided the inspirational model for Suzlon's entry into the big league. Tanti explains:

"Reliance because they think big and execute fast; Tata because it has always contributed to the society and country's economy; and Infosys because it has created opportunities for the young talent of the country and shared its wealth among them. I wanted my company to be an amalgamation of these three respected giants.

"We now have the momentum to manage the growth. Our whole mindset is established on high growth. All processes and systems are geared towards it. There is no risk because the market demand is there. Global warming is a concern growing all the time. We have to grow faster to mitigate the risk. It is clearly not just business, but contributing to the future and helping our future generations. That is the reason I am able to attract a lot of good talent. People want to be part of this type of growth."

Business

Wind energy has certain advantages over other sources of power. A single windmill can be set up in a matter of weeks, far less than the time taken for nuclear, hydroelectric, or coal-based power plants. Unlike thermal power, no fuel cost is involved and it can also be installed under water, in the sea. Most importantly, it does not release any pollutants.

Wind energy does come with drawbacks, however, as it can be unpredictable and has a low plant load factor (the ratio of average output to maximum capacity).

Tanti experienced the unpredictability of international demand for wind turbines when Edison International, California's largest utility owner, canceled its order option in 2008. That is among a string of events that made it a very difficult year for the company. While Suzlon should have been reaping the benefits of a world hungry for clean energy, the credit crunch sent its stock plummeting. The turbulence hit the company hard and Suzlon's share price crashed 90 percent, reducing the value of the Tanti family's stake to £830 million.

Nevertheless, he is unfazed by this minor setback:

> "Actually, the Edison cancelation has turned out to be good for both of us. With the first phase delayed because of cracked blades, we would not have been able to execute the second phase of installing an additional 300 MW capacity for Edison in the prescribed time. Edison would have suffered because of that. Since neither of us was comfortable with the situation, it was best they called it off. So there have been no financial damages. Our relationship with Edison remains a good one."

In developed markets, there is a conscious decision to reduce dependence on fossil fuels in generating energy to lessen carbon dioxide emissions. Developing countries like India are following suit. Tanti predicts:

"If the target is that minimum 20 percent of all energy must come from wind, then we require 30 to 40 years. So within the wind energy sector, we don't see any competition. Slowly it will become more competitive than the conventional sources of power and margins will further increase."

Recognizing the huge brand equity that he's built up in Suzlon as a company providing solutions for climate change, Tanti has also started to look at blended clean energy solutions with solar energy and announced his plans in this respect on the sidelines of the World Economic Forum's "India Summit" in 2008.

Turning Point

In 2001 Tanti did some serious analysis and concluded that wind energy is one of the main industries of the future. He decided to create a new business model based on complete vertical integration. He explains:

"Earlier we were purchasing components and simply doing the assembly and selling of projects. We decided to become an end-to-end solution provider. This accelerated growth for the international market. The biggest advantage was that I could grow the way I want to. If I am dependent on my vendors and they are not growing, I can't grow.

"If I am growing faster than my vendor then their profit margin will increase, not mine. When the demand increases, he will charge more. This will create uncertainty. I wanted to grow faster than the market. The market is growing at 20 percent while we are growing at 80 percent. This was possible because of this strategic change.

"The customers are comfortable because we have a full value chain and they are assured delivery security, with new capacity across markets available to service Suzlon's and the industry's requirements. And they know if tomorrow any-thing goes wrong, the company has the ability to manage that product. So that change in our model has been the way we have achieved high growth."

Nevertheless, this high growth did not come easy. It was an uphill struggle for him to communicate and convince people of his vision:

"The first reaction was always that it is not possible. It took me a while to convince people that we have to do things dif-ferently from what we are used to because the target is more ambitious and the requirement is very high. People would think I am stupid. I urged them to at least start dreaming, thinking in that direction and then I can guide you on how to achieve this high growth."

Indian Perspective

For energy-hungry India, which imports two-thirds of its petro-leum needs, the oil price surge has produced a swelling trade deficit. A nation of 1.1 billion people, India is the world's fifth largest market in terms of annual capacity addition for wind power. Tanti believes that there is no other major renewable energy source that can compete with wind for India's needs:

"Indian thinking is always on a larger perspective. Whether something can be done or not is secondary. Indians tend to have a clear picture, direction, and vision for the future. We are very hard working. I've always said India is like an elephant, it starts slowly but once it gets running, no one can stop it."

He also vehemently denies the charge that India is not doing enough to tackle climate change:

"India is far ahead when it comes to climate change. This impression being portrayed that we are only consuming and not contributing is wrong. People are just not aware. Our forest cover is 20 percent higher than 10 years ago. We use just over 600 KWh per capita a year, among the lowest energy consumptions in the world. We don't have the luxury of excess, so we make optimum use of what is available.

"From day one, Indians have been recycling. We always find ways to reutilize our rubbish. By birth Indians have energy efficiency in their system. A small house will switch on just one bulb at night to keep their energy bills low.

"Even in wind power, India is the fifth largest after US, Germany, Spain, and China. Why is it not another developed country? Why is India ahead? Simply because we know our resources are limited and we learn to make the best use of them."

Charity

This hard-nosed business outlook stretches to the softer aspects of Indian society as well.

Named among the world's 100 eco-barons in the *Sunday Times'* Green Rich List for his green investments worth £648 million, Tanti hit the headlines in 2008 when it emerged that Suzlon fell into the third largest donor category ($1–5 billion) to the Clinton Foundation. At the Clinton Global Initiative that year, the company pledged that it would bring 3,500 MW of clean electricity to nearly 10 million people. This project would involve developing green energy-generation assets worth $5 billion over the next five years.

This confidence to be able to deliver goes hand in hand with an extremely people-centric approach. Suzlon has 250 human resource professionals working around the clock to find the right talent and training to distribute products efficiently. This extends to huge contributions in rural India. Areas without any electricity due to India's 16,000 MW power deficit have benefited from Suzlon wind farms. By the sheer logistics of location, they are the first to access energy from a new wind farm. Tanti explains:

"We take our corporate social responsibility very seriously. We take care of all aspects of a village's needs, their drinking water, education, hygiene, food, health, and medical. We provide full support for their surroundings. I strongly believe that the society around should also grow and become self-sustaining. We have 80 employees in CSR to see how best to implement this.

"We have 60 primary schools, where we take care of everything from infrastructure, books, training of teachers to periodical audits. I want to help develop the country for the future."

He strongly believes in India's growth potential, which he believes has not been completely fulfilled yet:

"We have the people, the minerals, none of our resources have been fully utilized. We have not leveraged our manufacturing base. Our biggest hurdle is infrastructure, but now that we are building it, we can achieve the high growth. In the next 20 years, India will be the highest growth country in the world. And I'm not just saying that because it's my country."

Family

Tanti does not intend to pass on the company automatically into the hands of his children. He explains:

"Both my children are graduates in finance. They don't have to take over the family business, just as I decided to set up my own. I will leave it up to them, whatever they want to do. And if they do want to set up their own business, the family will provide private equity for that. Suzlon will be run by a professional set-up. The size is so big that this is the most advisable way forward, than running it like a family business."

An extended family of 16 live together in a block of four rented flats in Pune. The profits he generates are meant for society rather than his own personal luxuries.

Like many Gujaratis, the Tantis lead an extremely simple, strictly non-alcoholic, and vegetarian existence. All important decisions are made at regular family meetings and conflict is avoided through delegation:

"Our family is run the same way as any organization. There is an added emotional value whereas business has just commercial value. Some discipline and code of conduct is a must and that needs to be reviewed and changed every now and then.

"We have regular meals together and have an annual family board meeting where all future plans are worked out. Each member's expertise is identified and he or she is put in charge of that aspect. We have our own farm, so one of my brothers takes care of that. No one member is competing with each other. We are all complementing each other."

But Tanti admits not being able to find enough time to spend with the family or on any pastimes. Whatever free time he gets is spent poring over technological magazines or the internet to keep himself abreast of new innovations. A vacation is rare, but when he does take one, he switches off from work entirely.

With none of the extravagances that come naturally to most billionaires, Tanti has a clear perspective on his mega bucks: "Wealth is not just paper value but how we share it out."

On a personal note, out of all those I've interviewed for this book, Tanti stands out for his energy. I was forewarned that he doesn't give many interviews and I had also heard that he wasn't a confident speaker, especially in English, but when I met him I realized that this couldn't have been further from the truth. I usually start my interviews by asking a simple question that normally elicits a brief and equally straightforward response, taking no more than a couple of minutes. Expecting the same with Tanti, I was pleasantly taken aback when I looked at my watch and clocked that his first response had taken 35 minutes. He has phenomenal energy that is driven by excitement and enthusiasm that are hard to match.

In conclusion, as a result of the credit crisis and a massive drop in sales, Suzlon's share price may have nose-dived; it may be cash strapped as a result of the business being so capital intensive; and the sector's reliance on bank finance may have brought Tanti to his knees, but his strategy to take the reins once more, divest assets, shift Suzlon's focus to Asian countries that offer incentives as part of their fiscal stimulus plans for green energy, and renegotiate loans underscores his commitment to the long game.

This energetic entrepreneur may be down at this point in time, but I'd caution anyone from betting against him, for the simple reason that anyone with such a phenomenal track record in entrepreneurship and such a passion to succeed is not going to be turned over that easily. As one of my other interviewees in this book said, a kite rises against the wind; in the same fashion, Tanti's rise on the global business scene is on track despite the challenges the world economy faces.

Shiv Nadar

- Founder of HCL and Chairman and Chief Strategy Officer of HCL Technologies, India's fourth largest IT company, employing over 60,000 people across 26 countries and generating revenues of over $2.6 billion.
- Ranked along with Facebook by *BusinessWeek* in 2008 as one of the Top 5 most influential companies to watch globally.
- Single-handedly responsible for stemming the criticism lashed out by trade unions in the West about valuable jobs being offshored to India.
- Named by *Forbes* in 2009 as one of "48 Heroes of Philanthropy" for endowing $30 million to provide affordable higher education in India and for offering $1 million in scholarships each year.

Right Place, Right Time

Shiv Nadar is India's biggest opportunist. I mean this in the nicest sense and by the end of this chapter, I hope you'll agree with my reasons for saying so.

You may think of him as a man who quit a steady job to sell calculators in India in the 1970s, as someone who grabbed a chance to unseat the mighty IBM, or even as a very wealthy person who came from a humble background and ended up as a major shareholder in a blockbuster firm that trains more IT professionals than all of India's colleges put together. All this in one man, who has very successfully spotted trends and interpreted situations in the hugely competitive global IT sector to generate significant returns for his shareholders.

At first, everyone thought that his ability of being in the right place at the right time was sheer coincidence, but as time has progressed Nadar has cultivated quite a following, who track his every move in the hope of replicating his phenomenal success.

The 64-year-old founder of one of India's first and largest information technology companies – Hindustan Computers Limited (HCL) – formed his firm in 1976 with few resources at a time when India had all of 250 computers. Amazingly, he also sold hardware and not the software that we associate with Indian IT firms. Let's remember that it is China that is meant to have mastered hardware, which makes Nadar's story very different from India's other software czars.

Over three decades, Nadar has created a globally recognized and respected company, and his uncanny foresight has propelled it to becoming a juggernaut worth over $5 billion. The company is a market leader, employing over 60,000 professionals with a global presence in 26 countries, including the US, Europe, Japan, and the Pacific rim. Over the years, HCL has become synonymous not only with computer hardware and software, but also IT education and technology development. Today it is one of the largest sellers of personal computers in India. It may be playing second fiddle to other Indian IT giants such as Infosys, TCS, and Wipro, but it punches way above its weight in the hardware market.

Global Vision

HCL commenced operations in the US in 1988, at a time when Nadar's peers were shying away from venturing abroad and "Brand India" was unknown. After establishing a strong base in the domestic market, he set his sights firmly beyond Indian shores – an approach that earned HCL the title of India's first transnational company in the IT sphere. Nadar says:

> "It was clear to me that the US is central to our achievements. It is a key market because even today the bulk of the technology originates from there. In the world of technology, it remains a very important place. So there was no doubt in my mind about entering the US."

HCL America was born in 1989 with its headquarters in Sunnyvale, California. The move was not an instant success, as the US was the toughest market to crack at the time, but this did not hinder its gradual progress. Today the company accounts for nearly 55 percent of HCL's worldwide consulting and IT services revenue. About the early challenges of globalization, Nadar recalls:

> "We started around the same time as Apple. It was a time when the size of a computer was almost like a table. In 1985 when we sold 100 computers in a month, it was a big event for us. But eventually everything is an anti-climax. The fun is in the climb. As the size of the computer shrank, our market horizons expanded. Nothing has ever stopped HCL from finding new marketplaces."

The company employed an inorganic growth strategy of acquisitions and joint ventures to create its global footprint and kicked off its expansion in 2001 by acquiring a controlling stake in Deutsche Bank's India software operation, Deutsche Software Limited (DSL). The deal included the 450 employees in the Bangalore operation and HCL made provision to acquire the remaining 49 percent over the next three years.

Toward the end of the same year, HCL consolidated its entry into business process outsourcing (BPO) services by acquiring a 90 percent stake in the Apollo Contact Centre in Northern Ireland, which it bought from British Telecom for $0.5 million. It acquired the remaining 10 percent in 2004. It made perfect business sense for some of the work the company had traditionally off-shored to India to be done closer to its clients, creating the concept of "near-shoring."

The purchase of the Belfast operation couldn't have come at a better time for HCL and the entire Indian BPO fraternity. At that time in the UK, trade unions like Amicus had picked a massive argument on the issue of "British jobs for British workers" and were lobbying aggressively for the Blair government to adopt a protectionist stance. At the peak of this very public debate, whether by sheer coincidence or by design, HCL provided the government with a perfect line to take. Here was an Indian company investing in British jobs for British people, and by doing so emphasizing, as Secretary of State for Trade and Industry Patricia Hewitt did many times, that "a job gained in India does not mean a job lost in Britain." The unions were forced to back down.

Nadar profited tremendously from being in the right place at the right time, and was personally recognized by Blair for his contribution to the UK–India bilateral trade and investment relationship. Nadar recalls:

"In BPO, our intrepid move to partner with British Telecom in a JV in Belfast made us the first to develop a global delivery model, before the term became fashionable from an

Indian IT services company standpoint. It also helped us to leapfrog into becoming the No. 3 player in BPO."

Since 2001, Nadar's vision and strategic planning have resulted in further expansion. HCL made a notable acquisition of Liberata Financial Services in 2008. Liberata, a BPO company with four delivery centers and 800 professionals in the UK, provided HCL with a deeper footprint in the financial services market, as it was a provider of administrative and customer services to the life and pension industry. Through this acquisition, at a stroke HCL took over management of over four million policies and records of clients including AXA, Barclays, and J P Morgan. Unsurprisingly, it plans to invest a further $24 million in Liberata over the next few years.

What emerged next would have been unthinkable only a short time ago. As a result of years of investment in relationships with corporate financiers and lawyers, when a company such as Axon comes onto the market, IBM or one of the big western players would catch wind of its intentions and pursue the firm doggedly to eventually take it over. For this reason, it came as a surprise to learn that Infosys, one of HCL's biggest competitors in India, was in advanced talks with Axon. Realizing the opportunity, Nadar jumped in, unafraid of taking on the might of Infosys to become the second bidder and snatch the company. Again, he demonstrated the sheer opportunism that has become his hallmark.

With Axon costing HCL $621 million, this acquisition was the largest undertaken by an Indian firm to date. What it added to the HCL armory was a greater ability to take on larger consultancy outfits like Deloitte, Cap Gemini, and Logica CMG in the lucrative SAP integration market. It is believed that for every dollar companies spend on SAP software, the systems integrators that install it can charge up to $5. With such logic supporting it, the Axon acquisition looks like a good bet, especially as Axon is already one of the world's largest integrators of SAP business software.

In 2008, prior to the Axon acquisition, HCL derived 29 percent of its $2 billion revenues from Europe, the second highest proportion among the Indian system integrators. Both the Liberata and Axon deals have provided it with the momentum it requires to take on some of the world's largest and most sophisticated IT projects.

Such acquisitions bring huge challenges, of which the integration of staff can be one of the biggest problems. Nadar recognizes that the people HCL employs are at the center of its universe. As a result, he encouraged a strong internal culture to develop, resulting in the "Employee First, Customer Second" policy, aimed at making the organization more accountable and transparent. This has been taken up as a slogan internally and its effects have been dissected by the *Harvard Business Review* and business schools around the world. Among its practices include the chance to take part in a weekly online opinion poll on key management decisions – those that have been taken already and those that are still to come. While the votes are unlikely to halt or reverse decisions, people do get a chance to register their views.

These unique management practices not only helped Axon and Liberata employees become an integral part of their parent company, they were a factor in HCL being given the prestigious Financial Times ArcelorMittal Boldness in Business Award in 2009.

Background

Nadar was born into a prominent trading community from Moolaipozhi village in the Tuticorin district of Tamil Nadu in 1946. His father, Sivasubramaniya Nadar, was a judge who was transferred from place to place within the South Indian state.

Shiv was one of seven brothers and sisters and thrived at school. He joined the PSG College of Technology in Coimbatore for a degree in Electrical and Electronics Engineering. He says:

"It was a fairly quiet childhood. I remember moving from place to place in Tamil Nadu, but they were all small towns. The first big city I saw was Chennai at the age of 22. I did well in studies and always managed to get scholarships. My streak of independence led me towards enterprise eventually while my other siblings went into journalism, law, and astronomy."

That fierce spirit of independence combined with his boundary-less thinking is clearly the mantra behind his success.

In 1968 Nadar moved to Delhi and started his career with Delhi Cloth and General Mills Limited (DCM), the fourth largest company in India at the time. He quickly earned a lot of respect within the organization for his hard work and enterprise. Along with a few colleagues, he pioneered the company's entry into IT hardware with DCM Data Products. The move was eventually to pave the way for his future initiatives.

Of his early career Nadar says:

"Back then India and its economy were not so open. For a young trainee to rise up in a company's ranks was a very uncommon thing. But my chemistry with the boss was always very good. He felt I communicated and articulated well. He was naturally very upset when I decided to leave and felt that I could achieve all my goals by staying with DCM, but my reasons for leaving were similar to Bill Gates – I envisaged a new world out there. He felt let down but we stayed in touch and he recognized that at the end of the day I had achieved something good for the country as a whole."

Business

Nadar was joined by five other DCM colleagues – Ajai Chowdhry, Arjun Malhotra, Subhash Arora, Yogesh Vaidya, and D S Puri – in setting up Microcomp to sell teledigital calculators branded as Micro2200. The group went on to create HCL in 1976 out of one room in Delhi. The unused *harsaati* (rooftop room) belonged to the grandmother of a friend and was extremely underequipped, but the six young men had big plans for it. What I found encouraging was that even today, despite most of them having retired or moved on from HCL, they remain in contact and enjoy vacations together around the world, such as during the Cricket World Cup in the Caribbean.

In 1976, HCL started by signing a distribution arrangement with Toshiba for its copiers. It went on to develop India's first indigenous microchip computer in 1978, at the same time as Apple and three years before IBM's PC. In 1980, it introduced a 16-bit processor-based computer to the market and by 1986 the efforts had begun to bear fruit, with HCL becoming India's largest IT company. Nadar points out proudly:

"Those days we thought there must be a space for personal computers, and there were several groups of people that went into building a personal computer. One was Apple, one was us, and there were several others. Early 1978, we started shipping out those computers. And there were only two of those that finally survived. One is HCL, which has got a bit more than half a billion in size facing India, and the other is Apple, which is around 2 billion in size. All the rest are gone."

Turning Point

With democracy taking shape slowly in India, the ousting of Prime Minister Indira Gandhi from office in the late 1970s brought with it an unexpected turn of events. The new socialist government, with no real understanding of the forces that shaped global commerce, sought to tighten the rules and by doing so forced international firms like IBM to exit India. Sensing this opportunity, Nadar went into overdrive to fill the gap that had been created. He explains:

"There was a regulatory requirement in the 1970s under the Janata government at the time that the multinationals operating in India should dilute their shareholding of the Indian subsidiary. Also, the source code of the product should be on Indian soil, rules that have since been changed. IBM did not want to comply with these requirements. They announced their intention to leave India in August 1977. It was the same month when HCL announced its microprocessor-based computer system, called HCL 8C.

"Most of IBM's Unit Record Machines (URM) were on rental and would have required replacement and coincidentally HCL's products fitted that requirement. Imports were generally not allowed and hence HCL stepped into this marketplace. So our products became value replacements for IBM's very old ones. It worked out well for us."

This was a clear example of how with sheer grit and determination, Nadar was able to turn an obstacle into an eventual advantage. He adds:

"The biggest hurdle then was governmental regulations on imports. So what we could do was not determined by what was technically possible, but what the state would allow you to input. There were very severe restrictions in the late 1970s, so we had to argue technically, but at the same time they were amenable to technical discussions. They were all engineers, and it was my job to go and convince them technically that some of these parts should be allowed to be imported. If I were to take one single largest block, it was that.

"The second largest block was complete lack of any private equity support that is available in the Silicon Valley today. There were no venture capitalists in India. So, we had to run, generate the cash within the business itself, and grow."

From selling mainly hardware in the form of computers and office equipment, HCL eventually recognized the need to focus on IT software. In 1997, it spun its R&D outfit off into HCL Technologies. Nadar was well aware that HCL had entered the software services space relatively late compared with industry peers such as TCS, Infosys, and Wipro, who had by then already built large businesses. To beat the disadvantage, he mobilized strong teams of professionals and focused on buying up companies. Its acquisitions were driven by the objective of acquiring specific expertise or domain knowledge, as with its purchase of Bangalore-based avionic software company Shipara.

Today HCL's software expertise spreads across semiconductors, operating systems, automobiles, avionics and airborne systems, biomedical engineering, and wireless telecom technologies, among others. The entire conglomerate encompasses IT hardware manufacturing and distribution, systems integration, technology and software services, BPO, and infrastructure management.

Not content with providing services to traditional sectors such as manufacturing or financial services, HCL embarked on a path that led to investments in research and development so that it could provide expertise to the hugely profitable aerospace and defense sectors, both perceived as requiring cutting-edge technology.

As a result of its investments, its latest success story is in the field of proprietary technology, allowing it to offer image processing solutions for a whole range of applications, including high-resolution images from satellites. Such capabilities include processing images from unmanned aerial vehicles (UAVs); real-time video capture and image exploitation in surveillance and reconnaissance missions, done through the use of embedded technologies; enhanced fusion vision for situational awareness applications, and automatic vision inspection systems for quick inspection of components in manufacturing.

In 2008, HCL marked another first with a strategic global alliance with Xerox Corporation. This made it the first Indian provider to serve as a systems integrator for Xerox's managed print services offering, which helps companies control their office print environment to achieve continual cost savings and productivity gains. HCL now manages more than 600,000 desktops and supports seven million helpdesk contacts across the world.

Key Strategy

All of these different strands of Nadar's business are linked with one key factor – technology. In the IT world, where technology becomes obsolete on a regular basis, he is credited with creating technology cradles for incubating and developing new, high-potential, and cutting-edge technologies. He comments:

> "You have to stay paranoid. You don't know in which corner which one of your assumptions is going to go wrong. Any business goal is built on a set of assumptions, and you have to constantly test the assumption to see whether it stands valid today. If it doesn't stand valid today, what are the changes?
>
> "If you don't do this, businesses will fail, or fail to produce the results that we wanted them to get to. So it is important to be extremely restless, to achieve the goals. I suppose that is what should be for an entrepreneur. And once he comes out of the restlessness, in any case he should sell the company and go away."

This restlessness is clearly what keeps him going, even today. Rather appropriately, he is affectionately referred to as Magus, a Persian term meaning wizard, for his magical ability to conjure up whatever he desires, which seems the case when we look at the growth of his firm. It's also a reference to the magical quality he brings to a management style that relies heavily on delegation. He says:

> "Actually, I would use the word empowering. When I was working in DCM, something which they did extremely well was they empowered me to build their organization in the electronics business. And I did it well, and I had a lot of pride in doing what I was doing. We wanted to do more, so we stepped out to do more. I believe that that's the best culture that would make building a large organization viable and possible. Which is what we do and we do that quite well."

Charity

This focus on empowering young people goes further, into the field of education and research. With Bill Gates and Mahatma Gandhi as his role models, Nadar has become well known for his goal to provide world-class, research-oriented, quality education at an affordable price to every Indian, with the aim of raising living standards throughout the country.

Way back in 1981, he helped his wife Kiran and some friends set up the National Institute of Information Technology (NIIT), which acquired the reputation of turning young Indians into computer whizzes at a time when India was not known for its computing prowess. About his first forays into the world of education, Nadar says:

> "Once we found that we could produce computers, a huge cost element eating into our profit was training our customers. The marketplace produced computer engineers, but the education system did not produce people who could use computers.

"So we said, okay, now we have to have the job of creating the manpower that will be able to use the computers. We said if that's a restricting factor, can we remove that. So, one of our people who was working in the company as marketing manager at the time, Rajiv Thapar, came up with the idea that why don't we commercially sell computer education. It looked very difficult, but the hypothesis research showed that it would work."

Today, it is reckoned that NIIT produces more software professionals than the entire college network in India. If this is really the case, Nadar deserves his share of credit in taking India to a vastly different trajectory of growth than would have been the case without this development.

In 1996, he founded the SSN College of Engineering in Chennai in memory of his father. This was more a labor of love for this philanthropist. As a result of his golden touch, within a decade it has been recognized as the premier engineering institution in India. Nadar not only funds it but takes an active interest in the running of its scholarship scheme, which is aimed at the extremely poor. He explains:

"I am a product of education. My scholarships were possible because someone gave something somewhere, so it is my turn to give back to society a little. It gives me so much happiness to see this institution grow. The scholarships are aimed at people who face abject poverty. Many of them have gone on to work for the *Wall Street Journal* and other such prestigious institutions. It is a great feeling to see the students succeed.

"It is a very aspirational institute because aspirations are nobody's preserve. There are no budget restrictions when it comes to developing research. I am a global man, but these are some things I do because they are very close to my heart. The benefit from education is very tangible."

He has also founded the SSN School of Advanced Software Engineering, which, in association with Carnegie Mellon University in the US, offers a master's in software engineering and robotics. It is because of such endeavors that in 2009 *Forbes* recognized Nadar as one of its "48 Heroes of Philanthropy."

He is an executive board member of the Indian School of Business, a dream institution created by the best minds of the country's academic and corporate world to create future leaders.

Nadar's charitable leanings extend beyond education, with a foundation to support female children. As an active member of the Public Health Foundation of India, he also aims to influence public health policy in the country.

The dedication of this media-shy recluse has been acknowledged time and again by the Indian government, which awarded him the Padma Bhushan, one of the highest civilian honors, for his contribution to the IT industry and the public good. In 2009, he was also accorded the "Businessperson of the Year" award by the British Government for his pioneering investments in the UK. In 2005 he received the CNBC Business Excellence Award from the Prime Minister of India.

In 2008, *BusinessWeek* listed HCL among the top five most influential companies to watch out for, an achievement of which every one of the 60,000 employees at HCL is proud.

For someone who entered the *Forbes* list of billionaires in 2000 and is ranked 214th globally, money, surprisingly, continues to mean very little to Nadar. He says:

> "Money can be made to create great things, but I don't think it really means anything *per se*. If you want to empower people, give them the tools. There's enough entrepreneurship in India to take care of the rest."

China

Nadar sees China as an ally in all these aspects of India's growth. He comments:

> "I grew up in an India and Asia that were poor. Now we are in an Asia that is very prosperous. It is all coming together extremely well. It is a period of fun for all of us because the climb is always fun. Once you reach the summit it can be a bit of an anti-climax. So we must work together with China."

At its fourth annual global customer meeting in Florida, dubbed Unstructure 2008, HCL stressed the importance of China among the emerging markets of the world, which include Brazil, Russia, and Indonesia.

Future Proofing

New markets are even more crucial in the economic downturn, which has hit the IT industry hard. The Unstructure 2008 event attempted to look beyond the crisis to address concerns around climate change, which seemed a departure from the types of focus that other Indian IT companies were adopting. Nadar explains:

> "It is a very, very serious issue. It is realistic to accept that oil will run out sooner or later. It is a *fait accompli*. To find methods by which to generate alternate energy is an absolute urgency."

Unstructure 2008 underpinned HCL's Go Green Initiative, and was made a paper-free and carbon-neutral event by purchasing carbon credits from Carbonfund.org. The keynote address by former US Vice-President and 2007 Nobel Peace Prize winner Al Gore applauded the company's innovative ways of tackling the issue. As part of its commitment, HCL also arranged to plant 650 oak trees, roughly one for each guest, on 2.8 acres of land in the Western Himalayas to help sustain the natural habitat of the oak silk worm.

With an uncanny ability to forecast trends and create and exploit opportunities, Nadar has spearheaded a strategy of diversifying risk by spreading HCL's wings beyond the traditional boundaries of the IT world. By doing so, he has transformed the company into a global player that is poised to become a stronger contender in a future shaped by the internet and other developments.

Unlike many other billionaires, what sets him apart is that he draws inspiration from completely diverse and unrelated fields, such as sports and arts. His unconventional conceptualizations are born out of the performing and fine arts, where preconceived notions are continually challenged. Furthermore, he attributes his sharp focus on goals and complete commitment to achievement to inspiration from top-level sportspeople. He comments:

"I'm a very avid watcher of many games, and some of the sportspeople have stayed my very good friends. And I have seen the passion to achieve a certain goal, and the goals are always a level of excellence. You know, they're all very well marked. And if you see an athlete, or if you see a sportsperson like [Australian cricketer] Shane Warne is today, they have very well-set benchmarks. They want to better them. They have competitors. It's almost like what you see, or what you deal with, in the business world. And in that, they go about with their game plan, to win."

Family

Nevertheless, in all this passion to succeed Nadar never forgets to take a break every now and then. His ideal way of celebrating a business milestone is to have a drink with his wife. His hard work has not turned him into a workaholic and he does manage to enjoy some holidays where he completely switches off. He says:

> "I do take a break. As a matter of fact, weekends I'm pretty much my own person, and at that time I spend time on myself, on my mind and my body, with my family, with my very good friends. I am a five-day, two-day kind of person. I enjoy spending time in my two homes outside India – London and California. I am often able to steer clear of computers and phones, a complete shutdown."

He laughingly narrates a time when he had decided to take a vacation after many months of work:

> "After switching off my computer, I asked my secretary to tell the senior team that I was not to be disturbed on vacation, unless there's a fire."

A senior colleague gave a rapid rebuttal:

> "You need not worry, if there's a fire, we'll be busy putting it out and not wasting time calling you for instructions."

Nadar knew that he had a team who looked on his company as their own.

His ability to switch off extends to some of his favorite pastimes, like gardening, reading, and playing bridge. He is also an avid film collector, with a vast international and Bollywood collection.

However, seeing him busy at his desk in his plush office in Delhi, surrounded by paintings from some of the world's best-known artists, it is obvious that he cannot completely give up his work either. He says:

> "Retirement is not on the map. I stepped away from the operations side of things long ago because I never enjoyed

190

that too much. But when it comes to leading from the front, I am there. Now I focus more and more time on things that give me personal satisfaction, like my philanthropic work. I stopped working for money a long time ago."

Nadar has continually pushed the boundaries by looking at different ways to expand and develop the company that he founded with six friends on a rooftop terrace in Delhi. He may have been helped by various circumstances out of his control, but his genius lies in recognizing the opportunity – whether it means unseating the mighty IBM, packing a call center in Belfast to the rafters with local employees, or coming from behind to acquire a firm that propelled the company into a different universe.

My interview with Nadar could easily have gone on and on had it not been for an appointment he had to keep with none other than the President of India. Nadar comes across as a man full of ideas, who isn't introverted but spends an extraordinary amount of time thinking about his decisions and deliberating on what the next wave of developments may be so that he can ride it.

Maybe now you'll understand why I feel he is an opportunist.

Baba Kalyani

- Chairman of $2.4 billion group, of which Bharat Forge is the flagship company.
- Bharat Forge supplies virtually every global OEM and Tier 1 supplier in the world, making it one of the globe's largest forgings companies.
- Recipient of global accolades and honors by esteemed institutions like *Forbes*.
- Spearheading a strategy to diversify into the energy, railway, marine, and aerospace sectors.
- An outdoorsman with a passion for thrill-seeking adventure sports.

India's Mr. Manufacturing

Baba N Kalyani has one very simple mantra in life – to be the very best in his business in the world.

This goal of world domination is not just a dream. The Chairman and Managing Director of Bharat Forge Limited (BFL), one of India's fastest-growing manufacturing firms, has turned it into reality with sheer hard work and determination.

It is no mean feat to be able to claim that almost every car made in Europe and North America – be it a Mercedes, a BMW, or a Volkswagen – contains a Bharat Forge part. Every second truck made in the US or Europe has a BFL front axle or engine component.

BFL has considerably grown its position to become the world's second largest forgings company. But in keeping with the turbulent times in the economy, BFL is rolling out a parallel process of diversification to shield itself from overdependence on a struggling automotive sector. It has set up a heavy forgings plant to cater to growth industries such as energy, railways, marine, and aerospace.

All this has been made possible thanks to one man's vision of cautious risk taking at a time when the Indian manufacturing industry was scoffed at as mediocre. Baba Saheb, as he is fondly referred to, took it upon himself to prove everyone wrong. He recalls:

"The manufacturing industry in India has been at the receiving end as a sector that produces shoddy products that are non-competitive. These were the kind of words hurled at us in the 1970s, 1980s and even early 1990s. I think that was the single most important factor that drove a little fire in me to say we will do something to prove this wrong and bring Indian manufacturing on the global map. That is how it all started 15 years ago."

193

Global Vision

Kalyani was almost single-handedly responsible for establishing the "Made in India" manufacturing brand as a force to reckon with in the global marketplace. He commenced his journey to global domination in 2003 with the acquisition of German company Carl Dan Peddinghaus (CDP), at a time when Indian entrepreneurial presence abroad was at best obscure. The company's global expansion spree can be seen as a perfect mirror of India's growing clout in the global market.

As India started booming, Kalyani found himself stuck in a catch-22. He needed to increase revenues to expand capacity, but was caught in a bind, as global auto manufacturers perceived the "Made in India" brand as inferior, which curtailed his ability to supply them with more of his products. He realized that by making an acquisition in a country like Germany, which was renowned for its engineering and manufacturing skills, he could make that the front end of his strategy and use it as a launchpad for global expansion.

Reliving the early days of his international expansion, Kalyani comments:

> "That first time I went and bought a company in Germany and saw all those Germans waiting to welcome me was my eureka moment. It was something completely inconceivable a few years ago that an Indian company could ever buy such a highly sophisticated and technologically advanced manufacturing unit in Europe.
>
> "There were natural hurdles to overcome. People were very hesitant to buy from an Indian company, as India was still seen as a country that did not understand manufacturing very well. There were inevitable rumors flying around that we would take work away to India. We not only proved everyone wrong by making the operations successful but also expanded them, adding many more jobs for the German economy."

Since then he's expanded his footprint with acquisitions such as Federal Forge, now known as Bharat Forge America; Imatra Kilsta in Sweden; Scottish Stampings; and a joint venture with FAW Corporation in China, now referred to as FAW Bharat Forge; and is all set to break into Latin America.

The reasons behind his phenomenal success are quite obvious. His factory in Pune, Maharashtra, is the world's largest and most technologically advanced forging facility, with a capacity of 365,000 tonnes. As a clear departure from the Indian norm, Kalyani employs mostly white-collar staff at every level of the business. He has been instrumental in reversing the trend of unskilled manual labor slogging behind technologically challenged machinery, instead employing skilled graduate staff trained in the world's most advanced processes.

In the unpredictable world of manufacturing, where demand for components varies on a year-to-year basis, BFL's figures speak for themselves. When most of his competitors were suffering the blows of a dip in domestic demand in the early 1990s, Kalyani boldly multiplied his production levels in anticipation of a surge in global demand.

BFL leapfrogged from a turnover of $100 million to $1 billion between 1997 and 2007. Its Chairman Kalyani, who made it to the *Forbes* list of millionaires in 2006 with a personal net worth of $1.4 billion, predicts that the company's turnover will increase substantially in the next few years. In sharp contrast, most of his global competitors are still struggling with turnovers of between $500 and $700 million.

It is this uncanny knack for business that sets him apart from others in his field. That is the reason he remains unrattled by the economic downturn and falling demand for components from struggling car manufacturers across the globe. He explains:

"Every automotive supplier is dealing with this cyclical downturn. Our strategy is to diversify into the non-automotive business and expand into supplying for large infrastructure projects in the field of railways, shipping and aircraft. Our sales to the Big Three are just around 2 percent, so we are well fortified in terms of market risk and have a diverse customer portfolio."

His intuitive ability to forecast predicts further stability in commodity prices and signs of recovery in the Indian auto sector by 2010, but he refuses to venture a guess on where the American economy is headed. He says:

"They did bring it upon themselves. The US has always spent more money than it earned and has always run on a negative savings rate. All kinds of things were lopsided but all this is the benefit of hindsight. When it was the good times, everyone was happy with its large consumption. I am very hopeful that President Obama will prove to be a force for good."

That force brings with it a great potential for BFL in the form of the Indo–US civilian nuclear agreement, for the simple reason that forgings form a major part of the construction of any nuclear plant.

Kalyani's diversification plans also include addressing the wind energy opportunity as Suzlon has done, with the establishment of wind farms in Germany and Sweden. Characteristically, he hopes to become a top five company internationally within the next five years, demonstrating his hunger to be the best at whatever he does.

This confidence is not misplaced when you check out the company's balance sheet for 2007–08, when its net sales jumped by 11 percent to Rs 46.5 billion.

Background

Born in 1949 to Sulochana and Neelkanth Kalyani, Baba Kalyani had an obsession with tinkering with machinery from the age of six. He would pull apart his bicycle only to put it back together again.

As he often proudly proclaims, his family's roots were in farming in the Satara district of Karad in Maharashtra. His grandfather, Annappa Kalyani, a one-time turmeric king, had insisted that his son shun the speculative nature of trading and concentrate on the security of agriculture. Following his advice, Neelkanth took up sugarcane cultivation on the family's 60-acre farm. He started one of India's first cooperatives, the Krishna Sahakari Sakhar Karkhana, and a land development bank.

However, Neelkanth could not ignore his industrial calling and in the 1960s he ventured into forgings on the advice of his close friend, industrialist S L Kirloskar (who continues to be one of Baba Kalyani's biggest role models, despite having passed away in the mid-1990s). The family moved to Pune as that was the hotbed of forging action, where the Kirloskars were making diesel engines and the Tatas were setting up a truck plant.

Back in those days, India's economy was a far cry from the dynamic set-up that is its trademark today. Every new industrial unit had to endure a long drawn-out process of acquiring licenses for manufacturing and importing machinery. Neelkanth underwent a series of struggles before the first forgings were produced at the Pune factory in 1966. It was these solid foundations that Baba Kalyani used to propel Bharat Forge onto the global stage.

During these formative times, the young Kalyani spent his vacations from the King George Royal Military Academy at Belgaum, which was a boarding school, at the Pune plant getting his hands dirty in the family business. His father appreciated this fascination with the family trade, not shared in equal measure by his other son, Gaurishanker, or daughter Sugandha. Having given up his education prematurely after his father's death, Neelkanth wanted the best education for Baba. After his graduation from BITS in Pilani, one of India's foremost science and technology colleges, Baba went on to one of the best in the world during his MSc at MIT in Boston. He recalls of his formative years:

"Boarding school taught me discipline. When you are in a military school, there is very little room to maneuver the system and I think that discipline has stood me in good stead all my life. It has made me a very simple, straightforward kind of person. That also gets me into trouble sometimes as I am too candid, but by and large I think people appreciate the openness and integrity behind it.

"Apart from the formal aspect of education, being at a top college like MIT creates a tremendous expansion in your thinking capability. It broadens your vision, increases your logic by a huge amount. The biggest thing I got out of my stint in the US was this ability to really think in three dimensions.

"As for machines, I was somehow always very mechanically minded. I liked machines right from my childhood, their feel, to be around them."

His love for machines drew him into the family business in 1972 and translates into a hands-on leadership style. On any given day when he is at his Pune factory, Baba Kalyani can be seen in the same company uniform as any other employee on the shop floor, getting his hands greasy just as he did as a teenager.

But it was not all work and no play during his student life. He loved the outdoors and was a regular on the tennis courts at MIT. This love of the outdoors combined with his thrill for speed shines through even today. He owns some of the biggest motorbikes produced, including a Harley-Davidson. He says:

"I have always been an outdoors person. When in college, I enjoyed motorboats, water-skiing, wind surfing, and motorbikes whenever I could get my hands on one. Of course, I have had accidents but that has never made me give anything up. I learnt flying for the same thrill. The whole process is amazing, when you first work on theory and then fly with an instructor. There is nothing that can thrill you more than your first solo flight. Once you have taken off the ground and are in the air, your heart is pumping, there can be no greater thrill."

Business

On his return from MIT, Kalyani got married to Sunita, a medical student, and set out to learn the ropes of the family business. It was a small company struggling under the weight of low technology and labor-intensive operations. Initially he was put in charge of sales, but he could see that unless BFL moved toward automation and robotics, there was no use trying to procure new orders.

He took charge of manufacturing and that is when his hard work began. The first and last on the shop floor, Kalyani used his ambition and drive to propel the struggling business into the twenty-first century. He says:

"That is the job of a leader. To run any business and lead a group of talented people, it is my job to communicate my dream and vision and make it theirs and to create enough passion and fire to make them achieve it. Everyone running an organization has certain aspirations. These are what dreams are made of. These dreams could be something as mundane as a patriotic feeling of doing something for your country or as sophisticated as wanting to be the best in your business in the world."

Kalyani Steel was set up in 1973 to make alloy steel for Bharat Forge, which forges components out of iron and steel. These components are formed into shape by heating at very high temperatures. The engine and chassis systems and components, including crankshafts, axle beams, steering knuckles, and other safety-critical components produced by this technique are high-strength materials.

BFL started out by focusing on making these "hidden" components for automobiles and gradually diversified into shipping and construction. It has a more than 35 percent share of the world market for certain products in the segment. All 2,000 of its products are on display at the Pune headquarters. The range of global customers also includes an impressive array of names like DaimlerChrysler, Ford, General Motors, Volkswagen, Toyota, Volvo, Renault, Dana, ArvinMeritor, Caterpillar, Cummins, and Iveco.

Its future expansion strategy involves moving into aerospace and power equipment. The Kalyani Group also has interests in wind energy, engineering steel, and specialty chemicals. Though the company had to scale down its growth predictions by 15–25 percent in the face of the credit crunch, being an old player in the game and having a diverse portfolio allows Baba Kalyani to remain upbeat during this downturn in the market.

Turning Point

The starting point of all this was a result of Kalyani's sheer confidence in the industry. In 1989, in what can only be described as a huge leap of faith, he took the decision to invest Rs 1 billion in technological upgrading at the BFL plant, when his company's worth was just Rs 1.5 billion.

Industry pundits, including his own father, were shocked with this company-threatening move and were left wondering whether he had lost his mind. After all, Neelkanth Kalyani would, quite naturally, not want to see a lifetime's worth of effort crumble in front of his own eyes.

The decision to double the company's capacity in a sluggish domestic market was Baba Kalyani's biggest gamble. Analysts were sure he was creating a white elephant, but he had his reasons. He had set his sights beyond the Indian market, as he explains:

"People thought I was nuts. Articles were written about this so-called white elephant... In the late 1980s, before liberalization, I realized we needed to do something different and bring in technology to drive our business forward. It required huge investment, but it was that one decision that took our company from being a non-entity to where we are today.

"I always felt we had the capability within our people to make modern technology work. At the time, bringing in robotics and making them work wasn't as commonplace in India as it is today. Largely because I am an engineer, have worked on machines, I have a feel of what can or can't be done. No one else took that chance at the time and the gap between us and our competitors is somewhere in the range of one to ten. I had enough faith to bet the company on it."

Neelkanth Kalyani retired in 1994. Today he is often quoted on the pride he feels at what his son has achieved, not only for the company but the industry as a whole.

Key Strategy

Baba Kalyani's gamble had paid off and he was now ready to take on the biggest and the best in the world. He began by targeting the North American market and in 1992 grabbed his first order worth $5 million from ArvinMeritor. The clincher was Bharat Forge's cost competitive pitch and high quality guarantee.

Soon it was time to venture into other lucrative world markets, as the automotive industry in both India and the US was facing a recession in the mid-1990s. The obvious choice was Europe, but that was to prove the hardest nut to crack.

That is when Kalyani's unique tactic of dual shoring was born. He explains:

"Our international strategy back in the mid-1990s was export oriented, because I could see that the domestic market was not big enough to meet our aspirations. But in Europe we had to first convince everyone of the India story and then make them comfortable about our company. That's when I went in for my first German acquisition. It was bought as a foothold that would help us build that trust relationship with customers, while using India as a back end set-up. It was a simple dual-shoring strategy for which we didn't go to McKinsey or anyone else.

"Once we built that trust among our customers, they were more confident and themselves suggested we make these products in India. Dual shoring is not all about cost competitiveness. The front end is kept next to the customers, using the same language and processes they are used to and the large manufacturing base is in a low-cost environment like India.

"Not everyone gets this balance right because they are getting the basics wrong. They tend to believe that price is the only important issue. But price is only one of many factors; there is engineering, product development, and, our biggest USP, speed. We pride ourselves in doing things in one-fourth the time than any existing supply chain and we have India's natural information technology at our disposal."

One of the key reasons for the success of this concept of dual shoring is Kalyani's very own integration technique. Instead of focusing on integrating business processes in two different continents and time zones, Baba went in with a people-focused approach. He realized that as long as he got the people side of the operations right, the business side would naturally fall into place.

He not only retains the local management, but triggers off a 100-day integration program after each acquisition during which top management from both countries meet up and discuss things, right from the basics of how to say hello and reply to an email. This addresses any cultural differences that could lead to barriers or mistrust in the future.

There is also a regular three-day company integration meeting every year in November, to which managers come with their partners to participate in team-building activities in an informal environment.

Kalyani's open-door policy at the swish factory just outside Pune keeps him in the loop of day-to-day operations. The strong work ethic among his staff is palpable as one takes the long-winded drive up to the gates of what is very much an Indian factory with an international edge. It brings to mind an army cantonment, harking back to Kalyani's military school upbringing. It is clear that the place has benefited from globally benchmarked practices, but combines these with the Indian value of fairness and an emphasis on human relations.

Indian Perspective

This is the unique Indian approach that Baba Kalyani brings to his global operations. Kalyani takes great pride in his Indian roots and explains:

"Indians tend to work with very people-led sensibilities. I am pretty sure a very structured and formal business set-up does not have the right effect. An India-led operation has two things going for it: one, by nature Indians are people focused and two, Indians have a tremendous sense of dealing with diversity. We deal with it on a daily basis. Everything is complicated and we learn how to make it simple. We have to deal with bad roads, poor infrastructure, the power going off. The West is not used to all this and wouldn't know what to do when faced with a situation out of the ordinary. Indians have some of the best brains, but we haven't had the opportunity to apply this until now because we didn't live in a high-tech manufacturing environment."

He has often spoken of his faith in the capability of young Indians to make their mark in the world. His biggest thrust has been on education, which he considers as key to the country's future. He set up his own engineering school in Pune to develop human capital. He also has a tie-up with Warwick University in the UK for a master's program, through which over 100 engineers graduate every year. He adds:

"I strongly believe that in terms of entrepreneurial and commercial capability, Indians are amongst the best in the world. We are taught right from childhood how to add and multiply. I have seen that someone from Europe is not able to grasp numbers as quickly as we Indians can.

"The way I see things developing in India, for about 50 years we were groping in the dark and working in a highly regulatory environment, without understanding what is really happening here or in the world. In the last 15 years a lot has changed. Businesses have reoriented themselves to reach out to markets everywhere. The next step is to convert this into value-added stuff. But creation of this wealth must go hand in hand with ensuring that the fruits of growth and development are dispersed and shared by all. And for this the single most important factor is education."

Charity

This strong belief in the power of education spills over into every aspect of Kalyani's life. He devotes considerable time to Pratham Pune Education Foundation, an educational charity that he founded and chairs. Pratham's aim is to provide primary education to needy children in the local community. He has never shirked his corporate social responsibility, and says:

"Education is something I feel very strongly about. It is the one thing that will make a difference to India's future. The philosophy behind Pratham is very simple: to create a process whereby we can bring dropouts and others left out of the education system back into the mainstream. Besides the money that the project needs, working with these kids brings you back to the ground level. One can get so busy in an air-conditioned office or flying around all over the world. It is nice to come back to the ground and see what the reality is."

This responsibility extends further into a green strategy that Kalyani unveiled in 2008. Bharat Forge is one of the few companies that can claim to be all green in its energy usage in the near future, largely due to the Chairman's plan to set up windmills for energy production.

China

It is this kind of forward thinking that has helped Kalyani prove the world wrong in its view that Indian manufacturing plays second fiddle to China. Instead of being overawed by the might of India's fast-galloping neighbor, he pulled off a coup of sorts with a joint venture with the state-run First Auto Works. BFL now has a 52 percent stake in China's largest automotive group. Kalyani says:

"If we are to be number one, we must have a presence in the second largest auto market in the world. The choice was between a greenfield operation and a joint venture and we went with the latter as it was a less risky proposition, because it is beneficial to have a partner who knows the business. In my view the government of China has got a couple of things right. It has fixed the infrastructure pretty well and used foreign investments as a means to create a market. Now that internal market is so strong that it is driving an entire economy."

While the Chinese economy is on an upward swing, the Indian economy is going through a downward phase in the field of manufacturing. But Baba is unnerved by this fluctuation. As he predicts:

"Forgings is a cyclical business globally, but at the same time it has long-term stability based simply on the sheer number of vehicles being built in the world. That will only keep increasing. What is important is to have a global strategy that does not limit your business to any particular market or company."

Future Proofing

This strategy of having a diverse portfolio of customers makes BFL one of the most risk-reduced businesses in the industry. It has a customer base of 40, none of whom accounts for more than 10 percent of the business. They range over three different geographies – America, Europe, and Asia – and each has a spread of at least two or three different segments. As a result, the Chairman's foresight has insulated the company from the unpredictable and cyclical nature of the business.

While no company can ensure complete future proofing, Kalyani's strategy of continually exploring new markets in

Mexico, and Brazil plays a part in achieving this goal. His 7,000 employees worldwide, including those in India, are mostly college graduates, who are able to leverage their skills and know-how to improve quality and focus on new product development. He says:

> "There is no option but to be up-front in technology and constantly move up the value chain. When we started exporting our products, we were seen simply as a low-cost provider. But once we established our footprint we became development partners. Today we command worldwide respect as one of the best. I have grown along with the company, having spent more than 22 years as a plant manager."

Family

It is this same lesson of working your way up that he expects his son and heir apparent, Amit Kalyani, to follow. He is candid in asserting that there are no guarantees of Amit naturally stepping into his father's shoes unless he proves himself worthy.

Amit, an engineer from Bucknell University, took to the shop floor in 2000. He is now Executive Director, a board-level position, responsible for overseas operations. Father and son share a passion for cars and the business and are unable to switch off from manufacturing even at the dinner table, much to the annoyance of Amit's wife Deeksha.

Most evenings at the Kalyani household in Pune's Kalyaninagar suburb are very family oriented. When at home, Baba Kalyani can be found in his study with his wife Sunita, his grandchildren, and his pet Great Dane Kaizer.

It is these strong family ties that set an Indian businessman apart from the world and Kalyani counts this as one of his biggest strengths. As he often says:

"They are my support system and I greatly value their love, care, and understanding, without which I would not have achieved even a measure of the success that has come my way."

And it is his favorite Chinese proverb that sums up his life and achievements:

"Happiness is someone to love, something to do and something to hope for."

As I drove out of the Bharat Forge complex, I reflected on how impressive Baba Kalyani's achievements are. The man came across as someone totally determined to make the most of everything he had to reach the apex of the highest summit in the world. That meant investing Rs 1 billion in technology when his company was worth a mere Rs 1.5 billion, and by having the confidence to acquire a start-of-the-art German competitor when his firm and sector in India suffered from a not-so-wholesome reputation.

More than anything, what stands out for me is his ability to bet the family silver on his own calculations. I know that I wouldn't bet against him.

Conclusion

The shock value of India becoming the economic epicenter of the world has subsided drastically over the past few years, for the simple reason that we realize that India can not only play the game but can, in fact, provide leadership on critical issues. At the same time, I believe that India is becoming more open to constructive criticism from outside, a sure sign of its positive and increasingly mature attitude.

In this conclusion I want to consider the main overall factors behind the success stories outlined in this book.

Made in India

That the Indian element is crucial is undeniable. Irrespective of the fact that Mahatma Gandhi is a role model for many, all these entrepreneurs are united in measuring their success in terms of the country's status on the world map. To varying degrees, they are also all devoted to corporate social responsibility.

Whether it's setting up a foundation, allocating chunks of profit to social issues, or simply taking time out for a cause close to their heart, they are keen to take India to the next level of social development. And this will prove the clinching factor behind the country's true progress, because the government alone cannot make that jump. It has to be with the help of the corporate world that some of the sticking points of infrastructural improvement and alleviation of poverty are addressed.

According to Harvard Business School Professor Tarun Khanna:

"It is more to do with the ambience. When you have large cases of deprivation in the backdrop, you have to be sensitive to that and do a lot more for the environment."

209

Kamal Nath, India's former Minister for Commerce and Industry, who was a powerful voice at every global economic summit from the World Trade Organization to Davos, attributes India's success to the capacity to "adopt and adapt." He says:

> "It is an Indian genetic trait that we have always been a country that has looked at ways to get the maximum out of the minimum. Indian management has a genius of its own. It makes things more efficient. They just need to sell their success story more. The mindset that questions what Indian companies can do is outdated. Minds take a long time to change."

This fire to prove the world wrong sets India's corporate ambitions apart from those of the rest of the world. The path to creating a true Indian multinational firm may be a bumpy one, but the toughest part of the distance has already been covered. The rest of the hurdles will smoothen out as the country gradually moves away from being a low-cost provider of goods and services to becoming a world-class one. It has struggled to shrug off the cheap and cheerful low-cost tag, but the inevitable move up the value chain is well on its way, as is evident in most of the companies profiled.

Taking a contrarian view, Suhel Seth, Managing Partner of Counselage India, dismisses the argument that India has a different take on globalization. He explains:

> "Globalization is not about an Indian company going abroad, but a company that happens to be from India working abroad without mishmashing the culture. You are not going there and planting the Indian flag. You are actually going there and planting values that the company or group will be driven by."

He provides the example of the Tatas and says:

"Wherever they have gone the culture of that company has been interwoven with that of the group. Being Indian matters only to a bunch of jokers sitting in India who live vicariously through other people they think have conquered the world. I don't think there is a place for nationalism in the modern economic world. It is irrelevant whether you are Indian or not, what is important is are you globally competitive, are you culturally and morally honest."

Climate Change

Nevertheless, that should in no way blind us to some important elements in which India is lagging behind. There is no common corporate voice emerging on the issue of climate change and the need for growing economies like India to take the lead in pursuit of a greener tomorrow. Surprisingly, there is even an element of denial, with some like Subhash Chandra stressing India's relatively miniscule contribution to global warming.

Suhel Seth, a friend of A-list Indian business leaders, says:

"Indian business does not care about climate change. It pays lip service to issues that are not to do with their core business. It is riddled with greed and tunnel vision."

The Indian perspective on the issue may be understandable given that it has a lot more pressing problems to deal with and that its per capita footprint is very small compared to the US and Europe. But it is a reality that Indian companies will have to address in the near future if their global victory is to prove a sustainable one.

Each of the entrepreneurs, professionals, and business leaders in this book deals with this issue in their own way, with Baba Kalyani and Tulsi Tanti actually basing the future fortunes of their empire on taking the potential of wind and solar energy to the world.

The Chinese Threat

In many cases, these leaders took on an impossible challenge, like Kiran Mazumdar-Shaw who started out with just $250 as investment. But they went on not only to multiply profits but also to build brands of which the country can be proud. They have made mistakes and taken decisions that have not always gone the way they were expected to, but the way in which each of them coped with the setbacks and in fact turned them around to their advantage is where the lessons for the future lie.

That is also what will define whether India takes the lead in Asia – China or no China.

Harvard professor Tarun Khanna, author of *Billions of Entrepreneurs: How China and India are Reshaping Their Future and Yours*, stresses:

"In China, it is very difficult to be an organization without the government being in your face. India is the opposite. It is open to ideas. India's view on China has also undergone a transformation from the searing memory of the 1962 conflict and is closer to a rational one. It is now seen as a country with which economic symbiosis might be achieved, even though security considerations remain important. India has more than the ability to speak English going for it. The degree of openness and transparency is the most important factor. In the long term, the Indian economy will be much more sound."

Several of the leaders I interviewed already had a "China strategy." Whether that meant setting up a captive unit to service their global clients or entering into a joint venture to manufacture goods, they have already engaged their so-called enemy.

Women in Business

India is now a place where an increasing number of women are climbing the corporate ladder. Whether it's in the software services industry or in auto parts manufacturing, or the merit-based system at ICICI that has resulted in Chanda Kochhar taking the mantle of CEO, women are definitely on the move in India's business world.

In particular, Suhel Seth describes Kiran Mazumdar-Shaw as:

"outstanding, humane and [a woman] whose human values are reflected in the manner in which she does business. She made women stand tall."

The Future of Family-Owned Businesses

Known to champion the interests of family businesses, India has seen somewhat of a shift in executive management and ownership, in that the larger businesses like Reliance and Tata have slowly begun to employ professional CEOs to grow their operations. Companies like Suzlon and Infosys, where the owner still holds a large shareholding, also prefer their future generations to run their own races.

This view is supported by Baba Kalyani, who refuses to accept that his son Amit is the only contender for the top job, or Tulsi Tanti, who sees his role increasingly as a shareholder and not in any executive manner. In the end, Malvinder Singh may have provided the biggest pointer to the future of family-owned businesses in India by selling his family's stake altogether.

Economic Crisis

I wrote this book in the grip of one of the worst economic crises the world has faced in living memory. There have been countless doomsday predications of the collapse of capitalism as we know it.

Maybe that is where Narayana Murthy's extraordinary theory of "compassionate capitalism" becomes all the more important. That India is better placed to tackle the global economic crash may be a sign of the resilience of its business leaders, who built their empires against a backdrop of grave challenges and social deprivation.

Grant Thornton's *India Watch* series points out that the culture of India is "value for money" oriented, which is a direct result of a large population underserved in many of the essentials of life. At the same time, it is also increasingly affected by changes in the developed world in a variety of fields. India may need basic sanitation and may lack cold storage for food produce, but at the same time it is the fastest-growing mobile market in the world. India embraces old and new ideas with equal fervor.

Hence companies that focus on delivering value at attractive price points are a more scalable proposition than those that seek to charge a premium for better quality.

Mark Kobayashi-Hillary of the National Outsourcing Association comments:

"Indian IT is dependent on the global supply chain and on other companies, so there will definitely be some impact of the global financial crisis, but the extent is hard to predict. In the short term they are taking a knock, but it is quite likely that they will come out of the downturn faster than their customers."

My Top 10 Learning Points

Apart from uncovering their thinking on the key themes above, it is valuable to list the top 10 lessons I've personally learnt as a result of meeting these captains of industry. They can be summarized in terms of the traits outlined below.

Ethics

Narayana Murthy would be the first to agree that he's a normal human being, one who is as likely to make mistakes as the next person. However, what impressed me thoroughly about him was his commitment to transparency, fairness, and ethics. We hear so often of Indian firms in which the baton is never passed on, but Murthy relinquished his position when the time came and ensured a seamless transition to Nandan Nilekani.

Take the Satyam scandal in 2008 as another example. Murthy ensured that Satyam didn't sink by refusing to recruit those who wanted to jump ship. With skilled software developers as its biggest asset, Murthy could have brought Satyam to its knees, given the sorry state the company was already in.

It is such exemplary behavior and personal leadership on diverse issues that mark him out. If there's one man who teaches us to walk the walk, Murthy qualifies in abundance.

Big picture

Shiv Nadar stands out as a "big-picture" man. Like some of the others he started his venture with very little, but he's stolen a march when it comes to being disruptive. Whether we take HCL setting up a call center in Northern Ireland and confounding vociferous critics of the IT outsourcing industry, or its ambition to acquire the leading SAP consultancy in Europe, Nadar has demonstrated time and time again the necessity to push the boundaries.

One of his initial moves was to realize that despite the company's first-mover advantage in hardware, it had lost ground to its Indian competitors in the software services market. Once the penny dropped, Nadar embarked on a strategy to shape the market to his advantage.

Objectivity

Putting aside everything you may read in the papers or on the internet, Malvinder Singh's ability to ignore any emotional baggage to arrive at objective decisions has to be his single biggest virtue. In a land where family businesses still prosper, Singh was accused by his peers and commentators of "selling the family silver" when he relinquished his family's stake in Ranbaxy to a Japanese pharma major. When asked for the reasons, he quite simply explained that Ranbaxy would not be able under its own steam to scale the heights that it could with the resources made available by Daiichi Sankyo.

After pocketing over $4 billion from the sale, we can be assured that Singh will emerge as a market leader in any business sector he chooses. With money alone he could achieve significant scale, but he also has age and attitude on his side.

Entrepreneurial zeal

What I can only describe as a masterclass in entrepreneurship, my interview with Tulsi Tanti motivated me more than most. You can differ with most people on a lot of things, but I don't believe anyone who knows him would disagree with my observation that Tanti's confidence in applying common sense to business decisions is what has resulted in the success he enjoys at Suzlon.

Whether we take his decision to enter the wind turbine market or his acquisition of major European firms that he integrated vertically, his logic in growing his enterprise is simple and obvious. Coupled with his trademark passion and energy, Tanti has created an industry in India that the likes of Baba Kalyani are now making a beeline to embrace.

Scale

Subramaniam Ramadorai will have retired by the time this book is published, but his achievements are noteworthy for future generations to learn. Take the simple fact that during his tenure, the organization he led, TCS, has integrated around 120,000 more people into its structure. Even given the sheer complexity of managing staff of all different nationalities in a huge number of countries, Ramadorai scaled up his organization to take a top 10 position in the global IT services market.

In an industry that is reliant on human and intellectual capital, Ramadorai has embraced those who are arguably more talented than himself to create a cash cow for the Tata group, which is proving invaluable in the cash crisis as a result of the debt taken on to acquire Jaguar Land Rover.

Belief

Kishore Lulla represents the kind of belief held by all those I interviewed. It is his belief that Indian cinema and soft power will bring acceptability of all things Indian to far-flung corners of the world. In its typically over-the-top cinema hits, with several costume changes and colorful song-and-dance sequences, he is being rewarded for believing that India's time has come.

Bollywood isn't just packing cinema complexes the world over but is also offering its high-tech, talent-rich technical expertise to Hollywood studios, the majority of whom are now taking advantage of the cost and quality advantages. Lulla's belief is vindicated by the tie-up of Anil Ambani and Steven Spielberg to explore such synergies.

With the internet revolutionizing the customer experience by allowing films to be downloaded to desktops, Lulla hasn't lost sight of the fact that it's the content and not technology that will drive the industry to new heights. Arguably, he could have taken a different route to make the most of the opportunities that arose, but his belief has anchored him to a sure path to success.

Persistence

Kiran Mazumdar-Shaw's story underscores the value of persistence. She could quite easily have packed everything in when she realized that her brewing career was not going to go any further, just because of her gender. She could have limited her growth, if she hadn't persisted in securing funding for her ideas. She could have decided not to become the midwife to an entirely new industry in India, had she realized that she was alone, but again, she persisted.

That same persistence has produced riches beyond her wildest dreams and her success has provided inspiration and ammunition to other women who have sought to shatter the glass ceiling in the corporate world. Her persistence in overcoming the toughest obstacles makes her stand head and shoulders above everyone else. India is a tough place, even today, so for Kiran to have emerged victorious is a case study worth understanding.

Confidence

The fact that he played the game of roulette and won defines Baba Kalyani's risk profile and character. In what he describes as taking a "leap of faith," he took a view, put his and everyone else's money where his mouth was, and in the face of family opposition, executed an ambitious plan to upgrade the technology in his factory in Pune. Twenty or so years on, he attributes his global domination to that same leap of faith.

It's easy to talk about this glibly, but just imagine the consequences had it gone wrong. If you're looking for a global leader with bags of confidence, Kalyani's your man.

Loyalty

K V Kamath is said to value loyalty above anything else. With a lifelong career at ICICI barring a short stint in Indonesia, the one thing he identified as a worrying concern was the short-termism of the company's young recruits. Known for his ability to develop the best and brightest bankers, through a natural process he has nurtured a high-performing team that has delivered exceptional results in a short span of time – a feat that he would agree would have been difficult to achieve had his team not had the long game in mind.

Sonjoy Chatterjee, Executive Director of ICICI, explains:

"Kamath is extremely well respected. People accept his advice not because of his position but because of his past record, the things he has done for India in general and banking in particular."

Ultimately, Kamath has created a meritocratic organization. At one time the entire top rung, except Kamath's own position, was occupied by female professionals, who had been rewarded not only for their skill and aptitude but because of the diverse experiences they brought to the board. And Chanda Kochhar has succeeded Kamath and become the first female CEO of an Indian bank.

Fearlessness

Against all the odds, Subhash Chandra saw an opportunity, pursued it relentlessly, fought opposition, and upset a lot of people, but emerged as the victor. Ultimately, Chandra's success has come about because he's done it his way and in his inimitable, fearless style. You wouldn't guess if you met him that he is one of India's most influential people, or for that matter that he has had the most prestigious accolades conferred on him, because he identifies more with the common man who fights the cause of the underdog than with playing the role of elder statesman and business leader, despite his mammoth achievements.

Final Word

This book is an attempt to sift through the jargon, dust off the myths, and spell out in simple terms what the future of India Inc. holds for the country itself and for the world at large.

The Tata group will most probably be the first Indian company to gain global acceptability on the same level as Coca-Cola, IBM, and Nike. But as Anshu Jain, Head of Global Markets at Deutsche Bank, explains:

> "The developed world has conquered using brands. India still doesn't have a super brand, but that is not particularly surprising because the Indian success story is only 20 years old."

There can be no doubt that we are at a defining moment that will determine the economic balance of the world in the near future. India will inevitably possess the key to global success, and the extent of its actual prowess will be determined to a significant degree by the fortunes and activities of the leaders and companies profiled in this book. With these entrepreneurs and firms shaking up new markets, the answer to the all-important question of whether these Indian companies are winning globally is a resounding yes.

Sources

In addition to personal interviews with the entrepreneurs profiled in this book, I consulted the following sources.

Narayana Murthy

Bachi Karkaria, "Narayana Murthy: The man who flattens the earth," in Anil Dharker (ed.), *Icons: Men and Woman who Shaped Today's India*, Lotus Collection, 2008.

North South Foundation, Transcript of speech delivered at New York University Stern School of Business, May 9, 2007.

Infosys.com, annual reports.

Subhash Chandra

Vir Sanghvi, *Men of Steel*, Roli Books, 2007.

Zeetelevision.com, annual reports.

Esselgroup.com.

http://timesofindia.indiatimes.com/business/india-business/Each-brother-to-own-70-80-of-business/articleshow/5150610.cms.

www.hollywoodreporter.com/hr/content_display/world/news/e3i4ac2561 838c4675c001b53f762219060.

Malvinder Singh

10th Global PWC Survey, pricewaterhousecoopers.com.

The Economic Times, September 6, 2007.

India Knowledge@Wharton, June 12, 2008.

Business Standard, April 13, 2009.

Ranbaxy Profile, ranbaxy.com.

K V Kamath

The Economic Times, October 3, 2008.

McKinsey on IT, Spring 2007.

ICICI Profile, icicibank.com.

Kiran Mazumdar-Shaw

Times of India reports, 2002–07.

India Today, August 9, 2004.
India Today International, June 19, 2006.
Financial Express, December 28, 2008.
Biocon.com.

Subramaniam Ramadorai
Business India Award Acceptance Speech, March 16, 2005.
TCS.com.

Kishore Lulla
Management Today, September 30, 2008.
Independent on Sunday, June 8, 2008.
Sunday Times, June 1, 2008.
Daily Telegraph, May 12, 2007.
PricewaterhouseCoopers, *Report on Indian Entertainment and Media Industry*, March 2008.
Erosplc.com, annual reports.

Tulsi Tanti
Rediff News, August 2008.
Times of India reports, 2006–07.
Business Today, November 16, 2006.
Suzlon.com.

Shiv Nadar
CNN.com, *TalkAsia*, December 14, 2005.
Business Today, October 26, 2003.
HCL Profile, hcl.in.
Baba Kalyani
Forging, January 1, 2008.
Business India, April 22, 2007.
India Unleashed, May 5, 2006.
Forbes.com.
Bharatforge.com.

Acknowledgments

First and foremost, I'd like to thank the entrepreneurs who agreed to participate in this endeavor. Although these exceptionally successful individuals are extremely busy, they were generous with their time and insights. In several instances, follow-up interviews were requested and generously granted. I'm grateful to all of you for allowing me the opportunity.

I owe a huge debt of gratitude to Sonjoy Chatterjee, Mark Kobayashi-Hillary, and Alpesh Patel. Once I had the idea for this book, they were the first friends I turned to for advice. Their encouragement, guidance, and active involvement are integral to my achievement.

I truly believe that the expert analysis, commentary, and insight provided by a wide range of people, including Ron Somers, Mohan Kaul, Hon. Kamal Nath MP, Anshu Jain, Gautam Kumra, the late Jayant Bhuyan, Hemendra Kothari, Subhanu Saxena, Karan Bilimoria, Suhel Seth, and Tarun Khanna, have contributed immensely to my thinking and ultimately to this book.

I'd also like to thank those who are often missed out but are hugely important in making things happen. Among these, I'd single out Charudatta Deshpande, Paula Sengupta, Bani Paintal Dhawan, Sarah Gideon, Madhvi Anant Jha, M Sundarajan, Vivek Kher, Sarita Iyer, Raghu Kochar, Czarina Nunes, Jeroo Tarapore, A G Pandu, Alex Crossman, Sunali Rohra, A S Lakshminarayanan, Anoop Kayarat, Roland Landers, Deepak Varghese, Rajeev Sawhney, and the Canary Wharf Group.

Thanks to the Saffron Chase and Chase India teams – Manoj Ladwa, Nikhil Khanna, Nitin Mantri, Sukhwinder Parmar, Deepti Patel, Pallab Sarker, Jill Richmond, and Kate Edwards – for the confidence they have shown in me.

To friends like Mandhese Samra, Aditi Khanna, and Anubrata Biswas for their critical and thought-provoking feedback.

To Nick Brealey and the team at Nicholas Brealey Publishing for challenging my thinking from the outset about the fundamental basis for this book. Their professional guidance and expert insight transformed the idea into a completed product.

Most importantly, to my family – Anya and Eesha, Tejal, and Mum – for their unconditional love and support.

Finally, I'd like to urge my daughters, as they grow older, to embrace their identity. We may live thousands of miles from India, but there's no escaping the simple fact that India is in our DNA. By embracing your Hindu faith and Indian origin, you'll actually become better world citizens, and you'll also be giving yourself a huge advantage in life. India's time has arrived!

Index

Abraham, John 157
Accenture 9, 24, 25, 120, 130, 139
Aditya Birla Group 6
Aegon 70
Ahuja, Vijay 156
Allen SpA 57
Amazon 144
Ambani, Anil 4, 85, 217
Ambani, Dhirubhai 3, 85
Ambani, Mukesh 3–4, 85
American Express 61, 121
Anil Dhirubhai Ambani Group (ADAG) 4
Apple 176, 181
Arcelor 6
Areva 162
Arogya Raksha Yojana 111
Arora, Ashok 21
Arora, Subhash 180
ArvinMeritor 200, 201
Asia Today 47
Asian Development Bank (ADB) 84, 96
AsiaSat 41, 46
Association of Women Entrepreneurs of Karnataka (AWAKE) 112
Astra Zeneca 68, 106
AXA 178
AxiCorp 101
Axon 23, 178–9

B4U 148, 155
Baaziger 148

Bachchan, Amitabh 47, 74, 148
Baghban 152
Bakrie Group 84
Bank of Madura 85
Barclays 178
Basics 56
Bayer 56, 58
BBC 44
BCCI 53
Be-Tabs Pharma 57
Bhai Mohan Singh Foundation 63
Bharat Forge 11, 192–208
Bharti Airtel 5
BioCare Pharmacies 111
Biocon 9, 98–117
Biocon Foundation 111
Birla, Kumar Mangalam 6
Blair, Tony 177
BMW 193
Board of Control for Cricket in India (BCCI) 49
Boeing 9
Bollywood 4, 9–10, 140–57, 217
Border 151
Boyle, Danny 152
Brain Trust of India 51
brand, "Made in India" 1, 2, 10, 92, 107, 194, 209–11
Branson, Richard 4, 11
Brar, D S 64
Bristol-Myers Squibb 106
Brockbank, Wayne 95
BskyB 144
BT 130, 177

Buch, Madhabi Puri 89
Buffett, Warren 11
business development
  Subhash Chandra 43–5
  K V Kamath 83–5
  Kishore Lulla 147–9
  Kiran Mazumdar-Shaw 104–5
  Narayana Murthy 23–5
  Shiv Nadar 180–81
  Subramaniam Ramadorai 124–8
  Tulsi R Tanti 167–8

Cap Gemini 178
Capita 130
Capital Bank 121
Cardinal Drugs 57
Carl Dan Peddinghaus 194
Caterpillar 200
Chandra, Subhash 8, 36–53, 211, 219–20
  background 42–3
  charity work 50–51
  development of business 43–5
  family 52–3
  global vision 38–41
  Indian perspective 48–50
  key strategy 47–8
  turning point 45–7
charity work 209
  Subhash Chandra 50–51
  Baba Kalyani 205
  K V Kamath 93
  Kishore Lulla 153–4
  Kiran Mazumdar-Shaw 111–13
  Narayana Murthy 31–3
  Shiv Nadar 185–7
  Subramaniam Ramadorai 135–6
  Malvinder Singh 72–3
  Tulsi R Tanti 170–72

Chatterjee, Sonjoy 90, 219
China perspective 212–13
  Baba Kalyani 206
  K V Kamath 94
  Kiran Mazumdar-Shaw 113–14
  Shiv Nadar 187–8
  Subramaniam Ramadorai 136–7
  Malvinder Singh 73
Chowdhry, Ajai 180
Cipla 60
Citibank 80, 121
Citigroup 132
climate change 1, 51, 168, 170, 188, 211–12
Clinton Foundation 171
Clinton, Bill 72
Clinton, Hillary 71
CNN 39, 44, 78
Coca-Cola 220
Comcast Corp 144
Confederation of Indian Industry (CII) 52, 84
corporate social responsibility 1, 93, 135–6
Corus 1–2, 121, 131
Crouching Tiger, Hidden Dragon 152
Cummins 200

Daewoo 118
Daiichi Sankyo 8, 59–61, 67–8, 73, 216
Daily News and Analysis (DNA) 36, 45
DaimlerChrysler 200
Dainik Bhaskar 45
Dana 200
DCM Data Products 180, 185
Delhi Cloth and General Mills Ltd 180

Deloitte 178
Deshpande, Jyoti 156
Deutsche Bank 177, 220
Deutsche Software Ltd 177
Diligenta 131
Dinesh, K 21
Disney 144, 150
Doordarshan 40
Dr Reddy's Laboratories 71
Dutta, J P 151

economic growth, India 1, 3
Edison International 167–8
EDS 130
Ekal Vidyalaya Foundation of
  India 50
Eli Lilly & Co. 56
Ericsson 121
Eros International 10, 140–57
Essel Group 37, 39
Essel Packaging 39, 43
EsselWorld 38, 39
Ethimed 57

family-owned businesses, future
  of 213
FAW Corporation 195
Federal Forge 195
Ferrari 9, 121–2
First Auto Works 206
Food Corporation of India (FCI)
  42
Ford Motor Company 2, 200
Formula 1 9, 121–2
Fortis Healthcare 69, 70
Fujitsu Siemens 139
future proofing
  Baba Kalyani 207
  K V Kamath 94–6
  Kishore Lulla 154–5
  Kiran Mazumdar-Shaw 115

Narayana Murthy 34
Shiv Nadar 188–9
Subramaniam Ramadorai 137
Malvinder Singh 74

Gandhi, Indira 42, 181
Gandhi, Mahatma 33, 138, 185,
  209
Gates, Bill 11, 88, 153–4, 185
General Electric 85, 121
General Motors 200
Ghulami 146
GlaxoSmithKline 57
global financial crisis 1, 214
Global Vipassana Foundation 51
global vision
  Subhash Chandra 38–41
  Baba Kalyani 194–6
  K V Kamath 78–82
  Kishore Lulla 142–5
  Kiran Mazumdar-Shaw 100–2
  Narayana Murthy 15–20
  Shiv Nadar 176–9
  Subramaniam Ramadorai 120–22
  Malvinder Singh 56–61
  Tulsi R Tanti 160–3
globalization 1, 108, 143–4, 146,
  202, 210–11
Google 143
Gopalakrishnan, Kris 21
Gore, Al 10, 160
Gupte, Lalita 89

Hansen Transmissions
  International 161–2
HCL Technologies 10, 23, 174–
  91, 215
Hewlett-Packard 10, 120
Hindustan Computers Ltd 175
Hindustan Lever 39
Hitchens, Harrison & Co. 70

IBM 9, 25, 27, 120, 130, 133, 139, 178, 181, 182, 191, 220
ICICI Bank 9, 76–97, 104–5, 213, 219
Imatra Kilsta 195
India Today 41
India
  economic growth 1, 3
  economic liberalization 11, 25–6
Indian Cricket League (ICL) 49–50
Indian perspective
  Subhash Chandra 48–50
  Baba Kalyani 204–5
  K V Kamath 91–2
  Kishore Lulla 150–53
  Kiran Mazumdar-Shaw 107–10
  Narayana Murthy 28–30
  Subramaniam Ramadorai 133–5
  Malvinder Singh 70–72
  Tulsi R Tanti 169–70
Indian Premier League (IPL) 5, 49–50, 139
Indian School of Business 187
Infosys Technologies 8, 12–35, 76, 166, 176, 178, 183, 213
Infosys Foundation 31
Iveco 200

Jaguar 2, 121, 131, 133
Jaguar Land Rover 118, 217
Jain, Anshu 220
John Deere & Co. 6
JP Morgan 178
Jupiter Biosciences 58

Kalyani Group 200
Kalyani Steel 200
Kalyani, Amit 207–8, 213

Kalyani, Annappa 197
Kalyani, Baba 11, 192–208, 212, 213, 217, 218
  background 197–9
  charity work 205
  China perspective 206
  family 207–8
  future proofing 207
  global vision 194–6
  Indian perspective 204–5
  key strategy 202–3
  turning point 200–201
Kalyani, Gaurishanker 197
Kalyani, Neelkanth 197, 201
Kalyani, Sugandha 197
Kalyani, Sulochana 197
Kalyani, Sunita 199, 208
Kamath, K V 9, 76–97, 219
  background 82–3
  charity work 93
  China perspective 94
  development of business 83–5
  family 96–7
  future proofing 94–6
  global vision 78–82
  Indian perspective 91–2
  key strategy 87–91
  turning point 85–7
Kamath, K Vishwanath 82
Kamath, Uma 82
Kaul, Mohan 11
Kaun Banega Crorepati? 47
key strategy
  Subhash Chandra 47–8
  Baba Kalyani 202–3
  K V Kamath 87–91
  Kiran Mazumdar-Shaw 106–7
  Shiv Nadar 184–5
  Subramaniam Ramadorai 131–3
  Malvinder Singh 69–70

Khan, Shah Rukh 82, 148, 157
Khanna, Tarun 8, 209, 212
Khanna, Tejender 65
Kingfisher 5
Kirloskar, S L 197
Kobayashi-Hillary, Mark 10, 214
Kochhar, Chanda 89, 95, 213,
 219
Kohli, F C 125
Krebs Biochemicals 58
Krishna Sahakari Sakhar Karkhana
 197
Kumra, Gautam 8

Land Rover 2, 121, 131, 133
Lehman Brothers 9, 80
Li Ka Shing 41
Li, Richard 41
Liberata Financial Services 178–9
Lionsgate 143
Logica CMG 178
Lombard 78
Lulla, Arjan 145
Lulla, Kishore 9–10, 140–57,
 217–18
 background 145–7
 charity work 153–4
 development of business 147–9
 family 155–6
 future proofing 154–5
 global vision 142–5
 Indian perspective 150–53
 turning point 149–50
Lulla, Sunil 156
Macmillan India 111
Macquarie 70
"Made in India" brand 1, 2, 10,
 92, 107, 194, 209–11
Madura Coats 116
Mahindra, Anand 6
Malhotra, Arjun 180

Mallya, Vijay 4–5, 102, 112–13
Martifer 162
Mazumdar-Shaw, Kiran 9, 98–
 117, 212, 213, 218
 background 102–4
 charity work 111–13
 China perspective 113–14
 development of business 104–5
 family 116–17
 future proofing 115
 global vision 100–2
 Indian perspective 107–10
 key strategy 106–7
 turning point 105–6
Mercedes 193
Merrill Lynch 63, 121
MICO 22
Microcomp 181
Mittal, Lakshmi N 6
Mittal, Sunil 5
Mody, Naval 125
Morgan Stanley 121
Movielink 144
MTN 5
Mundogen 57
Munnabhai 152
Murdoch, Rupert 8, 11, 45–7,
 53
Murthy, N R Narayana 8, 12–35,
 65, 214, 215
 background 20–22
 charity work 31–3
 development of business 23–5
 family 34–5
 future proofing 34
 global vision 15–20
 Indian perspective 28–30
 key strategy 27–8
 turning point 25–7
Murthy, Sudha 22

Nadar, Shiv 10, 174–91, 215–16
  background 179–80
  charity work 185–7
  China perspective 187–8
  development of business 180–81
  family 189–91
  future proofing 188–9
  global vision 176–9
  key strategy 184–5
  turning point 181–4
Nadar, Kiran 185
Nadar, Sivasubramaniya 179
Nandkarni, S S 83, 84
Nath, Kamal 210
National Health Service 130
Neopharma 101
News Corporation 45–7, 53
Nike 220
Nilekani, Nandan 21, 34, 215
Nortel 121
Novartis 9
Novelis 6
Novozymes 100

Obama, Barack 17–19, 196
Ohm Laboratories 56
Om Shanti Om 148, 157
Orchid Chemicals 58

Packer, Kerry 49
Padukone, Deepika 157
Patni Computer Systems 21
Pearl Assurance 131
Pfizer 66
Playwin Invest 45
Pratham Pune Education Foundation 205
Progeon 24
Prudential 78

Public Health Foundation of India 187
Puri, D S 180

Raghavan, N S 21
Ramadorai, Subramaniam 9, 118–39, 217
  background 122–4
  charity work 135–6
  China perspective 136–7
  development of business 124–8
  family 138–9
  future proofing 137
  global vision 120–22
  Indian perspective 133–5
  key strategy 131–3
  turning point 128–31
Ramadorai, Mala 138
Ranbaxy 8, 54–74, 216
Rao, N Rama 20
Reliance 3–4, 166, 213
Reliance Capital 4
Reliance Communications 4
Reliance Entertainment 4
Religare 54, 69–70
Renault 200
REpower 162–3
Reserve Bank of India 85
Rextar 64
Roshan, Hrithik 148
Royal Bank of Scotland 80

Samsung 118
Satellite Television Asia Region (STAR) 41, 46–7, 48
Satyam Computer Services 6, 17, 133, 215
Saxena, Subhanu 9
Schwarz Pharma 59
Scottish Stampings 195
Sen, Amartya 23

Seth, Suhel 211, 213
Sharma, Shikha 89
Shaw, John 116
Shetty, Devi 111
Shibulal, S D 21
Shipara 183
Singh, Analjit 63
Singh, Bhai Mohan 62, 63
Singh, Malvinder 8, 54–74, 213,
  216
  charity work 72–3
  China perspective 73
  family 74
  future proofing 74
  global vision 56–61
  Indian perspective 70–72
  key strategy 69¬–70
Singh, Gurbux 61–2
Singh, Harpal 65
Singh, Manjit 63
Singh, Nimmi 61, 63
Singh, Parvinder 56, 61, 62, 64,
  65, 74
Singh, Ranjit 61–2
Singh, Shivinder 65, 66, 69
Siticable 47
Slumdog Millionaire 10, 152–3
Sony 48, 143
Spielberg, Steven 4, 217
SSN College of Engineering 186
SSN School of Advanced
  Software Engineering 187
STAR Plus 47
State Bank of India 77
Sun Life of Canada 131
Suzlon Energy 158–73, 213, 216
Suzuki Motors 5
Syngene 106

TALEEM 50
Tanti, Tulsi R 10, 158–73, 212,

213, 216–17
  background 164–7
  charity work 170–72
  development of business 167–8
  family 172–3
  global vision 160–3
  Indian perspective 169–70
  turning point 168–9
Target Corporation 121
Tata Consultancy Services (TCS)
  9, 118–39, 176, 183, 217
Tata Group 1-3, 9, 118–19, 121,
  124, 130, 133, 166, 210–11,
  213, 220
Tata Motors 118
Tata Sons 136
Tata Steel 1
Tata, Jamsetji 2
Tata, Ratan 2, 118, 138
Tempest, Brian 65
Ten Sports 48
Terapia 57
Terapia Ranbaxy 72
Thapar, Rajiv 186
Times of India 41, 45, 53
Toyota 200

Unilever 39
United Breweries Group 4–5,
  102

Vaghul, Narayanan 84, 95, 104–5
Vaidya, Yogesh 180
Veria 44
Vision Group on Biotechnology
  112
Volkswagen 193, 200
Volvo 200

Wal-Mart 5
Walchand Group 22

Warner Bros 144
Welch, Jack 85
Whyte & Mackay 5
Wipro 23, 176, 183
women, equal opportunities for
  28, 89, 98–9, 109–10, 213

Xerox Corporation 184

YouTube 140, 143

Zee Café 43, 44
Zee Cinema 43, 48
Zee Entertainment Studios 48
Zee Limelight 48
Zee Motion Pictures 48
Zee Music 43
Zee News 43, 44–5
Zee Sports 43
Zee Studio 43
Zee Telefilms 43
Zee TV 8, 36–5
Zenotech Laboratories 57